Deliverance

Also by Michael Perry from SPCK:
The Paradox of Worship

THE CHRISTIAN EXORCISM STUDY GROUP

Deliverance

Psychic Disturbances and Occult Involvement

EDITED BY MICHAEL PERRY

First published in Great Britain 1987
SPCK
Holy Trinity Church
Marylebone Road
London NW1 4DU

British Library Cataloguing in Publication Data

Deliverance.
   1. Church of England   2. Exorcism
   I. Perry, Michael   II. Christian Exorcism
   Study Group
   265'.94   BX 5147.E9/

   ISBN 0–281–04261–6

Printed in Great Britain by
Latimer Trend & Company Ltd., Plymouth.

Contents

Acknowledgements

We are grateful to the following, who have allowed us to reproduce material from books published by them or material of which they control the copyright:

Morgan-Grampian (Professional Press) Ltd and the Editor of *The Practitioner* for an extract from 'Psychiatry and the Occult' by J. Guy Edwards and D. Gill in vol. 225 (January 1981); the Revd Douglas Howell-Everson for six pages from *A Handbook for Christian Exorcists*, privately published in 1982; Messrs T. & T. Clark and the Editor of *The Expository Times* for an extract from 'New Testament Exorcism and its Significance Today' by J. Keir Howard in vol. 96, no. 4 (1985); Messrs Darton, Longman and Todd, and Servant Publications, PO Box 8617, Ann Arbor, Michigan 48107, USA for an extract from *Renewal and the Powers of Darkness* © 1983 by Cardinal Léon-Joseph Suenens; Messrs Hodder and Stoughton Ltd for permission to reproduce several extracts from *Christ Triumphant* © 1985 by Graham H. Twelftree; the Church Society and the Editor of *The Churchman* for an extract from 'Demon Possession and Exorcism in the New Testament' by J. D. G. Dunn and G. Twelftree in vol. 94, no. 3 (1980); the Secretary of the Panel on Doctrine of the Church of Scotland for extracts from the *Report of the Working Party on Parapsychology* presented to the General Assembly in May 1976. Material contained on page 361 of the *Report of Proceedings* of the General Synod of the Church of England, vol. 6, no. 2 (July 1975) is reproduced by kind permission of the Central Board of Finance of the Church of England (CIO Publishing). The Liturgical Commission of the Church of the Province of South Africa has given permission to reproduce and adapt a considerable part of its draft report, dated October 1983, on the liturgy of exorcism.

Preface

The first letter of John (3.8) tells us that the Son of God appeared for the very purpose of undoing the devil's work. We believe that the Church exists for the same reason. The devil's work is manifold, and not all of it is obvious. The occult is but a small part of his empire, but it is there that many Christians need special guidance, and often feel out of their depth. Not everything that is popularly described as 'the occult' is properly so called, and many requests for the removal of evil spirits have to be refused because they are mistaken and inappropriate. Christians have a task of discernment as well as a task of action before they can discover the most effective way of proclaiming the lordship of Christ in any particular situation and making it real to those who are in trouble.

The Christian Exorcism Study Group has helped train those who advise Anglican bishops in this area, as well as members of other Churches, for a number of years now, and its members feel that the time has come to share its insights with a wider public. We are grateful to the Archdeacon of Durham for taking a mass of material – interim reports on particular aspects of the subject, notes made by various members, papers specifically written for this purpose – and welding it into a single volume. In its final form this has been discussed by a conference of representative members of the Group and endorsed by them as indicating the most useful approach to cases of various kinds.

The great majority of dioceses in the Church of England now have their bishops' advisers (or teams of advisers) in this area, and readers wishing for help in particular cases should approach them in the first place. The bishop, his secretary or chaplain will put any bona fide inquirer in touch. Other Churches will have their own arrangements.

✠ Mark Ludlow   President
(Canon) Dominic Walker OGS   Clerical Chairman
(Dr) David McDonald   Medical Chairman
(The Revd Dr) David Gill   Past Medical Chairman

Preface

Paul Sturgess	General Secretary/Treasurer
(The Revd) Douglas Howell-Everson	Conference Secretary
(The Revd) George Mitchell	Librarian

The Christian Exorcism Study Group
c/o The Churches' Council for Health and Healing
St Marylebone Parish Church
Marylebone Road
London NW1 5LT

April 1986

1

Deliverance

From time to time, the ministry of Christian exorcism flares into public prominence, and it is easy to take a glamorized view of it. Not only is the reality far less sensational than the picture which is presented by horror films and the largely fictional reports beloved of certain sections of the media, but exorcism is only one weapon in the Christian armoury of those who seek to bring the power of God to bear on those needing deliverance from bondage to the powers of sin and evil.

In 1972 the SPCK published the findings of a Commission on this subject which had been convened by the then Bishop of Exeter in 1965. The 'Exeter Report' in its printed form (*Exorcism*, edited by Dom Robert Petitpierre OSB) represented only the tip of a much greater mass of material and case studies collected by members of the Commission. After the Report had been published, some of the authors and contributors continued to meet as an informal body calling itself the Christian Exorcism Study Group. Its membership has changed over the years, but it has always aimed to include parish clergymen, theologians and medical practitioners (some of its members have belonged to more than one of these categories at the same time). It has not been a self-publicizing group but has, rather, preferred to work quietly away in the hopes that it could test out the conclusions of the Exeter Report in pastoral practice and see whether its experience would lead to any convergence of methods of approach, of diagnosis and of practice. We believe we have experienced such a convergence and that the time is now ripe to offer the results of our common endeavour to the Church at large.

Within the Church of England, nearly every diocese has its adviser (or team of advisers) in this ministry. This has come about partly as a response to the recommendation of the Exeter Report in 1972, and partly after a statement made by the then Archbishop of Canterbury on behalf of the House of Bishops in the General Synod of the Church of England in 1975. Members of the clergy, and others, look to the diocesan adviser for help in this ministry in a wide variety of situations where the presenting symptoms are psychic or occult in nature. Many parish priests

1

feel 'out of their depth' because they have no previous experience of such cases, or because they feel threatened by forces which they are not confident they can control. The adviser may help by coming in and taking the case over, but often it is better if he can counsel the parish priest so that the man on the spot can deal with it himself. Not only does this avoid the misconception that there is in the diocese a kind of magician who has access to sources of power that the 'ordinary' Christian (or even the 'ordinary' clergyman) cannot tap; it also helps to spread more widely the expertise that the adviser himself has built up over the years in dealing with similar cases. This book is offered in the same spirit. It is intended to help those who exercise primary pastoral care, to show them something of the range of cases they might expect to meet, and to help them exercise discernment.

The Exeter Report had the title *Exorcism*. We have entitled our book *Deliverance*, which is a much wider subject. Exorcism is a specific act of binding and releasing, performed on a person who is believed to be possessed by a non-human malevolent spirit. The word 'exorcism' may also be used for the spiritual cleansing of a place which is believed to be infested by the demonic. Deliverance is about freeing people from the bondage of Satan. It may occasionally involve exorcism, but generally it does not. It is important to reserve exorcism for those few cases where it is appropriate and necessary, and to use other methods of bringing the lordship of Christ to bear on people or places or situations which are troubled by the results of folly or unbelief or sin, or by the works of the devil, but are not actually 'possessed' by an evil spirit. Some Christians see every sin-laden situation as an opportunity to practise exorcism. That is as unhelpful and as much an over-reaction as the opposite error of denying the reality of the powers of evil and their capacity to hold human beings in thrall. What is most pastorally helpful and spiritually upbuilding is to find the appropriate treatment for each particular case. We hope the following pages will help.

2

Counsel for the counsellors

Every now and again, someone who is in trouble of a kind which has a 'psychic' or 'occult' component comes to a Christian for help. The range of presenting symptoms can be bewilderingly wide – it includes such phenomena as a sense of the continuing presence of a close relative who has recently died, apparitions of the dead, noises (such as rapping sounds) and/or unexplained movements of objects in a house, the sighting of 'ghosts' either once or repeatedly in the same place, personality changes after involvement with occult practices, the desire to break free of a group involved in Satanism or magic, or a host of other possibilities. Sometimes the key to the problem will be expressed in terms which speak of normal or excessive grief reactions, sometimes in terms of the psychological strains and stresses which distort relationships in a family or a work-group, sometimes in terms of the activity of human beings no longer physically on this earth, sometimes in terms of the direct work of Satan or of his subordinate demons. In this book we will attempt to bring some sort of order out of the mêlée of possible kinds of disturbance, and to suggest what have, in the experience of members of the Christian Exorcism Study Group, been the most helpful ways of ministering to each kind of manifestation. But first, some words of advice to the person who is trying to help.

This book is written to guide Christian ministers in pastoral situations. 'Ministers' may be priests or lay people; the people who come to them may be parishioners, friends, 'patients', or 'victims'. For want of a better set of terms, we will henceforth normally use the words 'counsellor' and 'client', as being the least emotive and most widely applicable. It is assumed always that the counsellor will be acting in our Lord's name as a member of the Christian Church on behalf of the Body of Christ, and that he is therefore working under the authority of the Church. In the case of the Anglican Church, this authority resides in the parish priest who has the cure of souls, or, where a major exorcism (see pp. 96–7 below) is to be undertaken, the bishop of the diocese. Other Churches will have their appropriate ecclesiastical authority.

The following guidelines should be borne in mind by all counsellors when faced with a case:

1   Treat every approach made to you seriously and listen with attentive care. The details of the client's story are sacred; your interpretation of them will depend on many factors. A carefully-taken case history will therefore be well repaid. The counsellor has a balance to strike – between questioning and notetaking to set the information in order, and listening empathically so as to encourage the client to give the account in his own words. There is a very real risk of prejudging the case and fitting it (at too early a stage) into neat categories predetermined by the counsellor. The only way to avoid this is to be scrupulous in aiming at a thorough grasp of the alleged happenings and how they are affecting the client. If this is the counsellor's prime aim, the client is unlikely to form the impression that he is not really being heard, whereas if the counsellor jumps in at too early a stage with his own interpretative comments, the client may well fear that his case has been prejudged and wrongly categorized. In any case, since the client is almost certainly considerably disturbed by what has been happening to him, and is possibly even in a state of terror about it; since he does not know what is going on, nor how seriously to treat it, nor how he is to obtain relief, the counsellor owes it to him to begin by listening carefully and – at first – with the minimum number of interruptions.

2   As you listen, pray inwardly for the person(s) concerned and for guidance for yourself. Make use of 'St Patrick's Breastplate' (see Appendix IV, page 134) or some similar prayer.

3   Keep calm. You are part of Christ's ministry of healing, commissioned (by baptism or ordination) to bring his peace to all situations, and kept under his protection. You are to bring peace and order out of fear, confusion and trouble.

4   Investigate, as far as possible, the social, family, medical and spiritual background of all concerned. Their ethnic background may predispose some people to believe with certainty in such things as curses or bewitchment in a way which may be foreign to your own outlook and seem to you to be superstitious. Similarly, the family background, if discussed in a low key, may disclose unusual tensions, or the medical details may reveal information about the use or abuse of hallucinatory drugs or such substances.

5   Remember that you are to act above all as a pastor, rather than as a judge.

6   Make careful notes of the case (see below, pp. 10–11). A comparison of these with what is said or done at a later stage may well reveal troubles and tensions not openly expressed. If you decide to call in the diocesan adviser, these notes will be invaluable to him.

7   If there is any question whatsoever in your own mind that the solution to the problem may have a medical or a psychiatric aspect, then call in appropriate professional help. If at all practicable, a joint ministry between priest and psychiatrist is to be aimed for (see pp. 118–19 below). Psychiatric care does not preclude a spiritual ministry – why else does the National Health Service pay to provide chaplains to psychiatric hospitals?

8   Above all, make the client feel that he is going to be welcomed and that he will be able to discuss things with you in a relaxed atmosphere. Never express shock or surprise at anything you are told. The object should be to reduce as far as possible the level of panic, and to reassert the reasonable and commonplace. One way or another, God – through Christ and his Church – is able to deal with this problem.

9   Ensure that where there has been involvement in ouija, tarot, or the occult or magic (whether ostensibly malign or benign), the person involved makes – at some appropriate stage – a formal and deliberate renunciation, and turns to Christ.

10   When you are able to make an initial (and perhaps provisional) diagnosis, and if the case seems straightforward, use the means at your disposal – prayer, laying-on of hands, anointing. If you are a priest, the strongest ministry you have is the celebration of the Eucharist, in which Christ's victory over sin and death is proclaimed and made real and effective.

11   Where more complex problems arise, or those which appear to you to involve demonic activity on a serious scale, do not attempt to tackle them on your own. Bring in a Christian friend or group, preferably through your diocesan adviser in these matters. As you prepare to confront the evil, ensure that there are other discreet and trusted Christians who are praying for you. Religious houses are used to responding to requests of this sort; the diocesan adviser will know whom he uses when he needs prayer support; and some bishops like to be

informed when their protective prayers are specially needed for a case in their own diocese.

12   Aftercare is vital. If a sympathetic Christian lay person, with some knowledge of this area, can be found to befriend the client, it can help him to feel less isolated and 'peculiar'. It is this sense of isolation and the lack of an understanding Christian friendship which so frequently drives people into spiritualist Churches. If it is at all possible, the 'follow-up' should include urging the client to see the problem as a call to a deeper spiritual commitment – not necessarily within the counsellor's own tradition. Whatever the counsellor's own views on the 'paranormal' or the 'psychic', it is a fact that many people have come to religious faith as a result of some such experience. It can be the means of breaking down a purely materialistic attitude and opening up levels of experience beyond the mundane, and the Christian counsellor should be aware of this. Especially in a Christian context, a problem with a paranormal or psychic element must be seen as far as possible as an opportunity for spiritual growth, and not merely as a temporary (and possibly pathological) aberration.

13   The above points give guidelines for immediate use when confronted with a client in distress. Over the longer term, we would advise counsellors:

(a)   to obtain some training in the recognition of types of behaviour malfunction and what spiritual, mental or psychic states they indicate;

(b)   to make use of the resources of the diocesan adviser (or team) and of the Christian Exorcism Study Group, to deepen their background knowledge;

(c)   to enable people to deepen their own spiritual life and thus become more effective instruments for the healing of their own neighbours;

(d)   to make use of the prayers of Christian communities in dealing with recurrent or widespread troubles;

(e)   to preach the gospel of Christ crucified and conquering at all times and in all places, so that all with whom they come into contact may be aware that there is no section of human life – joy or grief – where he is not;

(f)   to ensure that their own spiritual batteries are regularly recharged by retreats, quiet days and personal inward prayer and spiritual reading;

(g)   to ensure that difficult areas where problems may be expected to arise, are covered by regular prayer;

(h)   to train themselves in Christian recollection, so that at no time are they taken aback by anything that occurs.

Counsellors are in the front line of the battle between Christ and his enemies, and they are therefore in spiritual danger. Dangers are of many kinds – spiritual, physical, social. It is difficult to categorize them, as they tend to be particular to the individual; but if the counsellor is aware of the following areas of danger, he is less likely to fall foul of them:

1   The principal spiritual dangers (which may well be linked) are concentration on self and residual doubt of God's authority. The deadliest of sins is spiritual pride, which expresses itself in a feeling of personal self-confidence. Faced with a client, this can result in an attitude akin to, 'I am not as other men, since I am gifted with the Holy Spirit (for which, of course, I thank God); so, because I am not this publican here, I can deal with his problems.' It will rarely be as crudely expressed as this, but counsellors will recognize the danger signals (in others, if not in themselves) at a fair distance. Those who have been given the gift of discernment of spirits should beware of using it uncritically. It is sometimes possible to confuse it with feelings which are being transferred from the client. Doubt of the power or authority of God is also a temptation to many counsellors. God can do anything he wills, and therefore he will deal with any situation, no matter how complex, messy or horrible. He will, however, deal with it in his way, which may not necessarily be the same as ours.

2   It is dangerous to enthrone the powers of evil, and easy to accept the idea of a majestic, dark god of Evil, or of a powerful and beautiful fallen angel of Mephistophelean proportions. A better conception of demons should be of beings like spiritual bacilli which attack the soul and personality. There should be no fear in the approach of the exorcist – he is under the protection of the cross. Conversely, he should beware of the too casual approach of 'I have dealt with this sort of thing before; it is easy'. As with the surgeon before the operation, there is the need to keep infection at bay and to have a spiritual 'scrub-up' before the opera-

7

tion – in the form of prayer, recollection and the reception of the Eucharist.

3   There may be danger from psychical attacks from Satanist groups whose activities are threatened. This is probably rare, and can in any case not harm the person of prayer. However, counsellors who rely on their own powers, discernment and expertise rather than on the power of Christ could well be in danger.

4   There is need to keep a balance between the rational and the intuitive in the approach to diagnosis. The mind may be more powerful than the senses, but it is not wise to write down intuition as of no value. Some people are psychically sensitive and can be aware of what is going on at a level unperceived by those without that particular gift. They need, however, to be additionally careful not to rely solely on their intuitive feelings, since they are not infallible. Feelings and intuition need to be subordinate to reason as we minister. The mind, rather than the senses, should therefore be our mainstay.

5   Beware of the danger of a slide into a magical approach to diagnosis and treatment. Diagnosis should not rely upon such paraphernalia as divining-rods, pendulums, colour-changing jewels and other occultist objects. Similarly, there may be an overemphasis in treatment on things useful in themselves – crucifix, Bible, holy water, which are represen- tations of spiritual things – rather than on the spiritual reality himself, and a reliance on formulae rather than on prayer. There is a certain danger in 'putting God to the test' in demanding divine guidance by mechanical means, or expecting to be able to guarantee divine action through sacred objects.

6   Beware of finding demons because you are looking for them, or because the client believes they are involved. Beware of putting people into standard categories derived from the last case you were involved in. Beware of setting up as an amateur psychiatrist or doctor, rather than putting the skills of your own disciplines into the service of theirs if they should require it. Always go for the simplest answer that will explain what is going on, rather than the more complex one, even though you know that complexities may well arise.

7   A possessed person or one who is sick in mind may attempt a physical assault on the counsellor or on sacred objects near at hand, especially if his expectations have not been met. There is also the danger of assault by

angry witches or Satanists whose control over a client has been interrupted or broken. Many of these anti-Christian groups are on the fringe of the drugs scene and may have criminal associations. If this connexion is suspected, the police should be consulted. The Drugs Squad or Special Crimes Squad will be found to be most helpful and probably to have some understanding of the problems involved.

8   There is a danger of sexual temptation and/or of blackmail. Agents provocateurs or blackmailers' associates will never advertise themselves as such. When visiting a disturbed house, the presence of another member of the team is an almost complete protection, providing that the counsellor never goes into bedrooms or other possible places of compromise unaccompanied by a member of his team or by some neutral person or by the parish priest. Where blackmail is attempted, the police should be contacted immediately.

9   'Bringing work home' is not to be encouraged. A calm, clear, peaceful home life is essential to the counsellor, and it is usually a mistake for a husband and wife to work together, and especially to use the home for work. Wherever possible, interviews should take place in the client's own surroundings, or at an office location. Every counsellor should know who his diocesan adviser is and what his telephone number is, but it is a mistake to make this information too widely available. There is always the danger of persecution by the mentally sick, or by members of anti-Christian groups. Such people can make the home life of the counsellor intolerable by telephone harassment or even by doorstep abuse.

10   The media love a haunt or a ghost or a paranormal happening. Even a scripted statement can be subject to partial quotation and to the emphases which can be put on single words or phrases by unscrupulous sub-editors. Unless the counsellor is familiar with the ways of the media, he should use the words 'no comment' as his best protection against misrepresentation, and not be enticed into saying any other words whatever, when pressed to do so by reporters.

11   There is always a danger of failing to allow for the proper distribution of time. An exorcism should be short and sharp; God (even when he acts through sinful humans) does not require hours and hours of cajoling and repetitious formulae in order to expel evil. What needs time is not the exorcism but the diagnosis which may (or may not) lead to it, and the Christian after-care which follows. There is a temptation to rush

in and 'do something' to help. It is more useful to spend time collecting and assessing the evidence.

12   Keep careful notes of what has been said and what has been done. Beware the danger of skimping on this. Full and accurate notes are a protection for the counsellor if things go sour and he is accused of mismanaging the case (or worse). Sample headings for such notes are given at the end of this chapter.

All these warnings make it sound as if no one in his right mind is going to advise a client in the area of the psychic, the occult, or demonic attack. While it is true that this whole subject holds real dangers for the foolhardy, and no Christian should imagine himself cut out for it and enter it recklessly, unadvisedly, and without due care and attention, it is also true that there are many distressed persons in the world who can be helped by a Christian counsellor. Christians who find themselves being impelled into this ministry (frequently through force of circumstances rather than by conscious decision on their part to do so) should thank God for the ways in which he seems to be using them. They should realize that no Christian vocation is without its pitfalls, but they should rejoice in the opportunities that come their way of witnessing to the Christian gospel and setting forth Christ as Lord to those who so desperately need him.

Taking case notes

Some such headings as follow will be found to be of use in making notes of each case. Notes should always be kept in a safe place, preferably under lock and key. Clients need to be assured of the utmost confidentiality at all times. They should be told that their case will not be disclosed to anyone else without their consent. Even the sharing of the details with another team member should not take place without the client's prior permission. To fail in this is to endanger the forfeiting of the client's confidence.

   Name of client
   Address
   Date(s) and time(s) of interviews
   Age
   Single/living together/married/separated/divorced
   Spouse's name and age

Children's name(s) and age(s)

Description of house; history and locality; occupancy

Employment of client and spouse

Education

Religious affiliation

Presenting problem (in as much detail as possible)

Friends, enemies and family (alive and departed) – reactions and relationships

Health, etc. – sleep pattern, medication, drugs, alcohol, sexual life, pressures, anxieties, diet, menopause, senility, schizophrenia, psychotic dysfunction, epilepsy, neurosis, depression?

Previous involvement – occult, tarot, seances, ouija, astrology, fortune-tellers, faith-healers?

Action

Referrals

3

Poltergeist phenomena

According to the *Oxford English Dictionary*, a poltergeist is 'a spirit which makes its presence known by noises'. In the experience of the Christian Exorcism Study Group, it is the single most frequent cause of appeals to members of the Group for help. The client will almost invariably say that there is a ghost in the house which is causing trouble, and would the priest please come in and exorcize it? In members' experience, exorcism is never an appropriate cure for such cases (unless they are linked with other, malevolent, activity as described in chapter 9 below). The cause seems to lie almost totally within the people who live in the house (or who work in the business premises affected), and never with an independent entity or spirit. For that reason, the Group prefers the slightly more cumbrous term 'poltergeist phenomena' to the simpler 'poltergeist'.

There seem to be common patterns of characteristic phenomena in poltergeist disturbances, which show marked similarity in different cases. They may, however, be perceived differently and given different explanations depending on the cultural attitudes prevalent in a given area or country. Sometimes there may be unusual phenomena unique to a particular situation or individual. A poltergeist attack often begins with small noises such as bangs, rattles, knockings, thumps, or clicks. At first they are discounted as normal or coincidental, but then the family notices that something odd is afoot and begins to interpret them in terms of the personal activity of an unseen (and usually unwelcome) guest. They are no longer 'bumps', they are 'knocks' or 'raps', and often 'footsteps' crossing the room or heard through the ceiling and interpreted as sounds of a person in the room or corridor above. After that, the effects rise to a climax and may include any of the following:

(a) Rappings and knockings are very common.

(b) Objects may be seen to move of their own accord and in a bizarre way, defying the laws of motion and gravity, sailing in curved trajectories, or changing course at a sharp angle.

12

(c)   Usually, however, the movement itself is not observed, but only inferred from the results of it, so that the object is suddenly found in an unusual place only a second after it had been seen elsewhere.

(d)   Objects appearing from 'nowhere'.

(e)   Glass, furniture, crockery being broken – usually not as a direct result of poltergeist activity, but by falling from a shelf to which the poltergeist had moved it. Occasionally, glass may shatter spontaneously.

(f)   Doors being opened or closed; curtains billowing when there is no draught causing the movement.

(g)   Missiles directed at a person at great speed, but usually narrowly missing, and rarely causing physical harm. Objects may refuse to move when watched, as if 'shy', but will immediately move when the attention of the observer is momentarily distracted.

(h)   Water dripping or pools of water appearing.

(i)   Rarely, spontaneous combustion.

(j)   Cold spots and, rarely, smells.

(k)   Sounds of music or the jangling of bells.

(l)   Voices, or baby or childlike sounds such as sucking, smacking of lips, occasional crows or chuckles.

(m)   Very commonly, interference with electrical apparatus – lights switched on and off, domestic apparatus set in operation, record players and tape recorders made to fluctuate in speed, electric clocks working in reverse, telephones ringing for no reason, bells going haywire.

There is usually a rhythmic pattern to this type of haunt. The effects start in a low key, build up to a climax, and then die away. This 'time pattern' applies both to daily performance and to the long-term disturbance. The duration of the troubles can be as long as six months at a time, but it is more usually measured in weeks. Poltergeist phenomena which continue unabated for a year or more are highly unusual. The activity is essentially naughty, childish, a cry for help by demanding attention, and is not experienced as essentially evil or malevolent.

Strange smells are occasionally associated with this type of 'haunt', and there may also be unusual temperature gradients or 'cold spots' in the house either momentarily or recurrently or over an extended period. The smells may be pungent or vile, or sometimes pleasant and reminiscent of stories of the 'odour of sanctity'. The investigator should first look for a natural or physical explanation. If none is forthcoming, inquiry will normally show that the smell is associated with a person who has experienced a sudden shock or is encountering deep personal problems. The counsellor should attempt to ascertain when the phenomenon first appeared, and whether it is recurrent, constant, occasional, associated with particular dates and times, or a 'once only' manifestation. It is possible for quite overpowering smells to appear and disappear without apparent explanation. They are often hallucinatory (the sense of smell may be hallucinated, just as the sense of sight may be) and associated with anxiety or fear; they disappear when the person is able to receive counselling or find a resolution of his personal problems. Evil smells do not of themselves indicate the presence of evil spirits, though they may appear as a side-effect in association with malevolent activity.

'Cold spots' should be tested with a thermometer. If they have a physical explanation, the thermometer will show a lower reading than in the surrounding areas. If they are undetectable by the thermometer, another explanation must be sought. It may be that the phenomenon is hallucinatory, or that it is a subjective feeling caused by a telepathic or clairvoyant awareness of something odd about that part of the house. It may be that someone is projecting fear into a particular spot, or that memories of immoral events or of tragedies are associated with that particular part of the building.

Smells and cold spots are not characteristic of the 'pure' poltergeist case, but may occur when other types of disturbance have become mixed up with it.

Whether in the simple poltergeist case or the case with a more complex aetiology, however, the phenomena do always seem to focus on one particular individual or group, who – whether consciously or otherwise – acts as the epicentre for the disturbances. The poltergeist 'goes with its owner', so that the removal of the 'owner' will result in the cessation of the phenomena and his return will lead to its restarting. There may, however, be some element of delay, as if the discharge of poltergeist activity happens some little time after whatever it was that caused it.

Having heard the account of the disturbance, and having tried to establish as exactly as possible how much of what was alleged to have happened was observed and how much was inferred by the client, the counsellor will want to form some provisional hypothesis about what is happening and how it is caused. He will be wise to look for normal explanations in the first place, and to posit paranormal explanations only if he can find no possible or conceivable normal one. Have the normal sounds and movements in a house been misinterpreted as having been caused by discarnate personal activity, and has the household become so 'jittery' that its members are by now disposed to let their imagination run riot? How much have they actually seen and heard, and how much of their description is inference rather than observation? (For instance, did they *see* the ashtray move of its own accord off the mantelpiece, or did they only *hear* a sound, turn round, and see it crash into the fireplace below?)

Fraud, of course, is a possibility, and the Group has invented the nickname of 'phoneygeist' to describe such cases. In its experience, there seem to be at least two types of phoneygeist:

1 The total fraud, entirely the product of trickery or deception, either as a practical joke or performed in order to obtain some identifiable object – publicity, attention, money, rehousing in a more acceptable area of council property. Practical jokers are the plague of some families. There is a particular tendency to practical jokes in the eight- to twelve-year age range, and some people have never grown up.

2 True poltergeist phenomena are uncontrollable and are brought about without any conscious effort on the part of the person at the epicentre of the disturbance. It may, however, be possible to reproduce by deliberate skill or effort, what began as involuntary phenomena, so that the phenomena are reproduced, or extended, or continued – sometimes while the genuine article is still in evidence, more often after the phenomena have died away. There are parapsychologists who believe that some stage performers have genuine paranormal abilities but that, because they cannot produce them 'to order', they have learnt how to reproduce them at will by fraudulent means for purposes of showmanship. The average counsellor is, however, unlikely to meet a client like this. It is more likely that the person concerned was receiving welcome attention while the phenomena were spontaneous, does not like the prospect of losing that attention when the phenomena begin to die out, and starts a phoneygeist in order to retain or regain it.

Genuine phenomena are more likely to occur regardless of whether the owner is in the immediate vicinity, whereas the faked event usually requires the person to be present and to have the necessary opportunity. Most phoneygeists likely to come the way of normal counsellors are unimpressive and easily distinguished from the genuine case. The following is typical:

Case 1

The counsellor was called in by the local authority, via the parish priest concerned, to advise on the veracity of a reputed haunt in a council house. Terrifying apparitions were reported, as were noises, cold spots, bloodstains which appeared and vanished, threatening voices, and the usual knocks and movements of objects. There seemed to be no reason for all this paranormal activity, and questioning of individuals soon produced wide discrepancies in the stories told. There was a noticeable absence of real dread which would be expected in a family suffering such psychic persecution, and a mechanical repetition of the stories broke down at the unexpected question. Reference to council records showed that the family had been trying for some time to obtain a transfer to another estate. In view of the fact that the activity was of the sort described in popular fiction and not of the sort normally presented to the counsellor, it was finally decided that the 'haunt' was a manufactured one, and the council was so advised. At a later date the family was transferred. Subsequent tenants reported no phenomena.

Fraud, however, need not be conscious fraud. It is possible for poltergeist phenomena to be caused involuntarily through automatism, in which the person concerned has no conscious knowledge or memory of what he is doing. Automatism is a medical/psychiatric disorder, in which the patient carries out complex motor or sensory activity without his conscious direction, usually when in a dissociated state in which he is unaware of what he is doing and is unable to recollect his actions afterwards. Automatism cannot be treated by the well-meaning amateur, and if the counsellor suspects that this is the cause of a poltergeist outbreak to which he has been called, he should seek professional advice. The counselling and treatment which are necessary will have to be done at a level deeper than that at which an amateur can safely operate.

Where misinterpretation of normal events does not seem to be the explanation, and where conscious or unconscious fraud has been ruled out, with what explanations are we left? The experience of members of the Christian Exorcism Study Group is that poltergeist phenomena are invariably associated with stress in the household or working group concerned, and that release of the stress results in cessation of the phenomena. How this 'works' is a mystery, but it seems as if the phenomena are produced by some form of psychokinetic energy produced and programmed by the deep unconscious mind of the poltergeist 'owner', as a form of protest at, or discharge of, intolerable stresses on the conscious mind. The mental or emotional or psychic stress seems to focus at one point and there becomes transformed into physical energy which is manifested in terms of noises or the movement of objects or the malfunctioning of electronic equipment. The initial activity causes fright which causes more stress among a larger circle of persons, so that the whole thing feeds upon itself until the emotional energy which lies behind it has been burnt out and the activity then comes to an end. Sometimes the activity carries pointers as to the nature of the underlying stress; in one case which had sexual undertones, shoes and pointed ornaments were grouped into patterns suggesting sexual fantasies.

The explanation offered in the last paragraph, however, is only speculation. The reader for whom the psychokinetic transformation of emotional energy into physical energy is not on his list of acceptable possibilities will have to make his own explanation; all we ask is that it is not an explanation arrived at in contradiction of any of the facts of the case. The most obvious correlation within the data available on poltergeist disturbances is the link between emotional stress and the phenomena reported.

There seem to be predisposing features which lie behind poltergeist cases; for example, a change in lifestyle, puberty, menopause, sexual malfunction, a drastic change in personal relationship such as a death or a birth in the family, worries about employment, promotion, or threatened redundancy, stresses between the generations in a family or at work (especially if there is an adolescent present), or stresses within the marital relationship. There appear to be peaks at about the age of seven, and at puberty – particularly if there is an only child with uncaring parents. Retirement is another time at which the emotional stress may mount to such an extent that it discharges in the form of a poltergeist. Families deprived of spirituality and unable to transcend the psychic disturbance by committing the situation to God in prayer are obviously more susceptible.

A move to a new home is often a cause of initiation of poltergeist activity. The move can cause great disturbance to the whole family – the father changes his job, the mother has to find a new set of shops, the children go to new schools, all of them have to find new friends in the locality. In 1968 the then chief rehousing officer of a metropolitan authority commented that, though council housing accounted for only 32 per cent of families in the United Kingdom, 86 per cent of poltergeist cases occurred in council houses when the family had lived for less than six months in its new home. Places which put pressure on their inhabitants tend to be the foci of poltergeist activity, and although council accommodation may not outwardly appear to be a source of pressure, it may lack homeliness, and the anonymous bureaucracy of the council ownership of property means that tenants have no particular person to blame if things go wrong, whereas a private landlord would be a recognizable scapegoat. Also, there may be a social-class effect in that many people living in council housing may be less able to express their problems and either cope with them or obtain help in appropriate ways.

High-rise housing, where children are unable to play, and the family unit is isolated from the rest of the community, increases tension and is a typical living condition where poltergeist phenomena may become apparent.

Poltergeist activity can be reported, not only from houses, but also from factories, office premises and prisons – particularly among short-term prisoners serving sentences of less than, say, six months. They have also been reported from hospitals, but the Group knows of no incident involving a patient in a mental hospital. This may be because poltergeist activity is an outlet for energy produced by the sort of stress which would otherwise result in mental dysfunction. However alarming the activity of the poltergeist, it is at least preventing something far worse from happening!

Families subject to poltergeist activity tend to be spiritually deprived and may often resort to such spiritual practices as table-tapping, ouija and planchette. This tends to accentuate the emotional tension, particularly if the participant has a bad conscience about his involvement.

The taking of drugs may alter consciousness and upset the capacity to be able to cope with emotional stress.

Press and television interest, in its coverage of poltergeist cases, can increase the fear-response by emotionalism and sensationalism. So may the involvement of mediums, who tend to link the phenomena with the activity of departed spirits – in this case, a manifest misdiagnosis.

A few case studies will illustrate typical poltergeist phenomena, diagnoses and treatment.

Case 2

A young mother was experiencing severe poltergeist activity, which included the movement of objects, interference with radio, television and telephones. The family also frequently discovered the house 'ransacked' when they returned home, although plainly there had been no intruder. The woman had had a very traumatic childhood, and the death of her father had reactivated the pain of this period of her life. She was helped, through counselling, to re-experience the repressed pain and anger of her early traumas, triggered by her recent bereavement, which was also 'worked through' in the counselling sessions. As she became able to integrate these feelings, and also to recognize the link between the psychological stresses and the outburst of poltergeist activity, the household returned to normal, the poltergeist phenomena died down, and she resumed her normal way of life.

Case 3

A middle-class professional woman was experiencing a kind of poltergeist activity in which, where she had a pair of objects, frequently one of the pair would move or break. This activity also took place when she was out of the house, and her husband witnessed such happenings when visiting other people's houses with his wife, and also when out shopping with her. On investigation, it transpired that the wife had had a mastectomy six months previously, and she appeared to be unreconciled to having lost a breast. The movement of one object of which there was a pair was clearly symbolically linked with this. Some two years later, when secondary cancer was diagnosed, the same activity recurred, but this time it affected all kinds of objects, whether they were a pair or not. As she came to terms with having cancer, the poltergeist activity faded.

Case 4

A household in a working-class area of a London suburb complained of activity including the movement of objects, spontaneous combustion of Christmas decorations, and written messages appearing in various rooms of the house. On investigation, it was discovered that the unmarried son who lived in the house with his father had recently moved in his mistress and her daughter. The child had been taken away from her own father and had to come to terms with living in a new home with her mother's boyfriend and his father. She was unsettled at the school to which she had been transferred. The mother showed a biscuit tin full of handwritten messages, saying that the handwriting was not that of her daughter or of any other member of the household. It appeared to be that of a young child, and included such messages as 'look at me' and 'can't you see me, I'm here all the time'. Her mother had encouraged the child to look on the poltergeist as a 'spirit friend', and she was writing messages to the poltergeist and leaving paper and pencil for the replies. It would appear that the trauma which the child was experiencing was creating the poltergeist activity. The written messages were cries for attention from her own unconscious. Counselling enabled the family to become more aware of the child's distress and her need for additional loving support and attention during this period. In particular, the healing factor was the acceptance and tolerance of hurt and angry feelings, without fear of retribution or further disruption to the family. This proved to be a more helpful and positive way of dealing with them than the collusive defence of projecting them on to a 'spirit friend'.

Case 5

This case occurred in a small self-contained workshop, occupied by two partners and two journeymen, manufacturing small items of a specialized nature. The phenomena comprised, in the main, the removal and apportation of small tools and items while the premises were occupied, the finding of lighted cigarettes in various places difficult of access, the continual unbolting of a locked door, and the movement of heavy lighting equipment. These two last items were witnessed by the investigators. An inexplicable and frightening phenomenon was the arrival in the morning post of a package of work sent in, which on opening was discovered to contain an item which had disappeared from the workshop the same morning. The 'owner' of the poltergeist was found to be the principal partner, who was under severe mental pressure for a weakness which could have led to social obloquy. On facing up to his problem and confiding in his partner, the poltergeist activity ceased.

Case 6

In the kitchen of an inner-city hostel, glasses were being smashed, tins on shelves were rearranging themselves, a heavy jug moved into an adjoining room, a cold presence was felt, noises were heard, and an electric appliance turned itself on without being attached to a wall socket. The staff became progressively anxious and annoyed. Each of them was interviewed extensively. The tension produced by these events was having mildly hysterical side-effects in other parts of the hostel. The assurance that there was nothing to fear reduced the tension and the intensity of these events, but did not prevent their still happening occasionally. There was not enough time to work in depth through everyone's needs and problems. It was therefore decided to hold a Eucharist (the hostel being run by a Christian organization) at which the kitchen and non-kitchen staff would be present, and to bless the people and kitchen. It was also pointed out that while an occasional further incident might happen, eventually the activities would die down. Furthermore, it was advised that kitchen and other staff should focus not so much on each other as on God, by holding regular Bible study and prayer sessions together. They did so, and the phenomena abated.

Case 7

A husband and wife living in a flat (their grown-up children had left home) described how a vile smell appeared at five o'clock every evening and lasted for about two hours. The smell was so unbearable that they frequently had to leave the house. The local council had been asked to investigate. Workmen experienced the smell but despite moving floorboards, inspecting the attic and removing some of the plastering from the flat, they were not able to find an origin for the smell nor a reason why it should appear at the particular time it always did. The counsellor was told that the smell had been appearing for eighteen moths. Six months before it began the wife, who had been working as a cleaner in a students' hostel, had been cleaning the bathrooms and toilets and had found one toilet occupied. At five o'clock, when she was about to finish work, she went back to clean the previously-occupied toilet. It was still occupied. When she was unable to obtain a response from within, she used her master key to open the door and discovered that a student had hanged himself. She was questioned by the police until seven o'clock that evening. Her husband had refused to discuss the matter and she had never returned to work. The trauma of that experience was finding its outlet by creating the vile smell. As she received counselling and prayer, the smell gradually disappeared.

Case 8

The client was a craftsman, who worked with his wife (or live-in girlfriend?), two young women, and a boy, and he was complaining of footsteps on stairs, clothes moved and in two cases thrown in disarray around the room they were in. In addition the client and his wife had experienced the television set 'going mad' and changing itself from channel to channel. One evening he thought he had seen from outside a face looking down at him from one of the front upper rooms. Other experiences were then related. Some years previously, in other premises, he had been asked by someone whom he said was a black magician to make certain items, and warned not to make a duplicate set. He had disobeyed the prohibition, and found the extra set a week or two later reduced to ashes, with nothing else burnt. A second incident concerned a curio which had belonged to a nineteenth-century actress. He wanted to link all the present events with her; he believed she wanted to tell him something, and he was asking the counsellor to help him communicate. The counsellor refused, suspecting that what lay at the base of the disturbance was not the spirit of the actress but relationships between the client and his wife and/or previous partners. This diagnosis was refused by the client, and the counsellor left. About ten days later, on a second visit, the counsellor was told of further phenomena – dresses swinging without a draught or human interference, a lavatory self-flushing, a door which resisted efforts to open it for about five minutes. The client would not accept a poltergeist explanation and said he would call in a medium. A fortnight later, the counsellor learned that a medium had visited the premises, but fled out, collapsing, 'having never known such a concentration of evil in one place'. No mention of the actress. Subsequent attempts by the counsellor to make contact with the client failed, so the case is an unfinished one. The counsellor feels there are unresolved personal tensions about relationships which lie at the roots of this case and that the phenomena will recur until the client is able to open himself to accept and explore them.

On being called in to a poltergeist case, the counsellor should clearly state that his object is to restore peace, normality and tranquillity. He will first listen carefully to the client's story and try to establish what is alleged to have happened, and in what order, and within what time-scale. Before he can go much further, he will need to satisfy himself that the case is genuine. In considering this question, he will have the following points in mind:

1 Test the reported phenomena. Do they appear to be deliberately controlled or not?

2 What is the general attitude of the person(s) involved? Do they get satisfaction from the situation and wish the phenomena to continue, or do they genuinely wish to be rid of them? Have they something to gain by acceptance of the phenomena as genuine?

3 Are there any observations made by an independent witness, outside the group involved?

4 Check with the parish priest, doctor, local police, housing department, whether they know of any relevant facts.

5 Look for other conditions which could give a natural explanation of the phenomena. Among these are factors of a meteorological, geographical, structural/architectural, or chemical nature.

6 Apply common sense to the possibility of faking the phenomena. Assumptions should always be checked. In the case of alleged teleportation, is the object B which is found the same as the object A which disappeared, or is it simply a similar one which could have been planted? One should endeavour to work out *how* the phenomena could have been caused if trickery were involved. It might be worthwhile contacting a member of the Magic Circle for advice on the feasibility of particular phenomena being produced by trickery, sleight of hand, misdirection, or other techniques of deception.

7 There is a range of possible mechanical tests for the detection of fraudulent behaviour. They include closed-circuit television, flash

cameras, infra-red lighting equipment, tape recorder, and thermometer. These are more appropriate to an investigation by a team of professional psychical researchers than to a visit by an invited counsellor who is being asked to stop the phenomena from disturbing the client.

8   Note possible mental or physical disabilities of the people involved, which may relate to their reliability as witnesses. For example, instability or confusion, hearing defects, visual impairment, or medication, may result in misperception of reality. Is there evidence of excessive consumption or sudden withdrawal of alcohol or drugs? Has the client needed to consult his general practitioner (or a specialist) recently?

If, however, the counsellor rules out the 'phoneygeist', his object will then be to discover the 'owner' or epicentre of the disturbances, and to establish the cause of the mental stresses on him. During the counselling process, the following points may with advantage be borne in mind:

1   The counsellor (if he can accept this as a valid and possible way in which poltergeists may operate) may wish to explain to the persons or family concerned that the happenings which are disturbing them are caused by some kind of transformation into physical form of mental stress or energy, and that though the mechanism by which this might come about is a mystery to science, yet the fact that such things happen is well established. What is going on may be unusual, but it is by no means unique.

2   Point out that, although the epicentre of the disturbance is usually focused on a single person who is most probably unaware of his function within the whole constellation of happenings, this does not necessarily mean that the phenomena are caused by stresses solely within that individual. That person may be a carrier for stresses and tensions within the family or his group of close acquaintances, and it may be helpful to give these a wider discussion in joint counselling sessions.

3   Point out further that the 'poltergeist' is in itself incapable of inflicting spiritual harm on anyone or anything, that it is certainly not a demon or demonic, that the 'owner' is definitely not possessed by it, and that he is in no danger of suffering a mental breakdown because of what is going on around him.

4   The family concerned should be encouraged to treat 'it' as harmless, and to discuss its activities without fear or malice and in as light-hearted a

way as possible. It thrives on tension and fear and shrivels when normal relations are uppermost.

5   The family may also be assured that the phenomena are short-lived and will tend to die out as soon as the underlying tension is resolved.

6   Counselling is in most cases very effective. This need not be counselling of a specifically religious nature; often, the intervention of a marriage guidance counsellor can be particularly helpful. Persons do not necessarily require psychiatric treatment, though psychiatric investigation may sometimes be of value.

7   Even if the case seems a commonplace and trivial one to the counsellor, it is certainly not to the sufferers. Counsellors should always treat poltergeist cases with concerned seriousness and in such a way that the family cannot feel either patronized or contemptible. Whatever the facts of the case turn out to be, it is certain that here is an individual (and, more often, a whole family situation) which needs help. The presenting symptom may not be the underlying malaise, but it is the function of the counsellor to dig down to what is really causing the trouble, and to help the family concerned to deal with it at the root. He will not be able to do this if the family think the case is below his dignity to deal with, so the counsellor should allow it to be seen that he is himself anxious to increase his own knowledge and general experience by that particular case. The counsellor must find ways of reducing the tension without inferring that the matter is a trivial one. The family may be reassured by being told that poltergeists are examples of a well-known phenomenon, but the counsellor will if possible emphasize any interesting facets of the particular case he is involved in, which lift it out of the purely routine.

8   Exorcism is *not* appropriate, because there is no evil spirit to be cast out. The phenomena have been caused by a combination of stress, worry, fear and strained relationships. If these can be disentangled and examined, and if the client is a Christian believer, then there are many weapons in the Christian armoury which can be employed. The blessing of the house and/or of the family may well be appropriate. So also may be the use of confession and sacramental absolution, and the celebration of the Eucharist in the house with the family present, offering it with special intention for the healing of inter-personal relationships. An atmosphere of love and unity in the house can be helped if members of the family can be given instruction in prayers to say for each other and for themselves. But if the client has no understanding of the Christian faith, these

approaches may do more harm than good, because they can be taken in a magical way as 'spells' which can 'cure' a house of the troubles affecting it, instead of as methods by which the spiritual attitudes of the people who live there may be healed, hallowed and directed aright.

Finally, let it be said that this chapter has described the 'pure' poltergeist. Investigation in any particular instance may show that the counsellor has been called in to a 'mixed' case in which poltergeist phenomena may have been triggered off by stresses connected with place memories, involvement with the occult, or other types of paranormal activity. If so, the advice given in the preceding pages will need to be combined with that to be found in the following chapters.

4

'Ghosts' and place memories

The appearances of ghosts are well documented in history, and feature in folklore both ancient and contemporary. Certain buildings and places are reputed to have ghosts, and it is not an infrequent occurrence to encounter a person who claims to have seen one.

A recently bereaved person may see the apparition of the loved one he has just lost, or there may be what are termed by the parapsychologists 'crisis apparitions'; these are dealt with in the next chapter. The present chapter deals with ghosts which appear to be associated with a particular place rather than with a particular person.

Ghosts are seen by a cross-section of people and in a variety of situations. They are sometimes described as appearing to be solid, or semi-transparent or transparent, and to be dressed in a variety of costumes. Rarely do they speak.

The vast majority of ghosts are likely to be products of the imagination or projections from the unconscious mind. A few ghosts sighted may well be apparitions of the unquiet dead, and these too are described in the next chapter, as they have particular characteristics which mark them out.

The seeing of a ghost may indicate an inner problem, or some unresolved conflict or fear, and frequently the description of the ghost provides a clue for the counsellor. It is important to know the history of the person seeing the ghost as well as details of family environment and personal problems. People who see ghosts will sometimes describe other paranormal phenomena and so believe that they are possessed or under demonic attack. The counsellor should normally expect that a ghost is projected by a subject in need of pastoral and possibly psychological care, and should go on to consider a paranormal type of explanation only if the former understanding is seen to be inappropriate.

Projection (as a psychological term) refers to the process by which impulses, wishes, attitudes and other aspects of the self are unconsciously denied as belonging to the self and are attributed to someone else. In extreme cases this projection may be visually perceived in terms of a hallucination or 'ghost'; more often it is simply a psychological mechanism whereby external scapegoats are found and made to bear the blame for faults which really originate within the person who is blaming the scapegoat. More will be said about psychological projection in chapter 8, in the discussion on 'possession'.

There are, however, reports of sightings of 'ghosts' which do not come into the categories of subjective hallucinations, psychological projection, or fraud. The 'place memory' is one such phenomenon.

It seems as though certain places are associated with the appearance of ghosts or unexplained noises. These may be experienced by a wide range of different observers over a long period of time, so that the place can get the reputation of being 'haunted'. This differs from the poltergeist, where the phenomena are linked more with the people observing it (and in particular the 'focus' person) than with the place, where a change in occupancy leads to the cessation of the troubles, and where the phenomena rarely last for more than a few months at a time, but are fairly intense while they are active.

Place memories are simply what their name suggests – memories which have become attached to places in the past in such a way that they can be reactivated and replayed in the present. In themselves they are neither good nor evil, and are impersonal. They show no sign of intelligence, nor do they recognize or react to the persons who observe them. Frequently they simply mechanically repeat a particular action, or walk over a particular route, and disappear when they have completed it – as though they were no more than 'video-clips', not the real persons of whom the clips are images. They cannot therefore cause any harm to living human beings, though they often cause fear.

The phenomena can be visual or auditory, occasionally both. They seem to require the presence of a person who can be termed the 'projector'. The word 'projector' in this context is, perhaps, rather unfortunate, since it is not being used in the same sense as it was four or five paragraphs back. It does not refer to a psychological mechanism, and certainly does not intend any slight upon the person concerned. What it means is that there is a person in the vicinity who 'tunes in' to the place memory so that, when certain conditions (unspecified and difficult to understand) are fulfilled, the memory can be activated and the 'clip' will repeat itself. The projector, besides observing the place memory himself, may also be capable of transmitting it, as he perceives it, to some or all of the others present with him. When this happens, what the various observers see and/or hear may differ considerably in detail. It could be postulated that what is happening is that one person is, as it were, on the correct 'frequency' to pick up the 'vibrations' of memory (these terms are being used purely by analogy, and do not suggest that the memory is electro-magnetic in nature). He then retransmits the memory as he perceives it, by some form of psychological or telepathic contagion, so that the bystanders also experience disturbing phenomena of the same general type, but differing in perceived detail. (The above explanation is an attempt at rationalizing what is perceived in such a case. Those who cannot accept the explanation are asked to believe that the phenomenon occurs — as witness the cases which will follow in this chapter — and are invited to work out explanations of them which will fit in with their belief systems. Once more, experience is sacred, interpretation is free.)

The event from the past which has laid down the memory is frequently one of unhappiness or stress, or of a tragic event which happened at that place, or of some habitual action associated with that locality which was repeated over a long period. Sometimes the memory seems to lie dormant for a very long time until it is, so to speak, 'recharged' unintentionally by an incident of similar mental or emotional stress on the part of the projector. In such cases, there is the possibility of a link between poltergeist-type disturbances and place-memory haunts. The stress causing the poltergeist may recharge or reactivate the place memory, and two different kinds of phenomena may become mixed up in the single case.

Place memories gradually fade out. Although traces of some have been observed which relate to events of more than 400 years ago, most are much more recent than that.

Case 9

This was witnessed once only by a farmer in a milking-shed. He had no previous belief in anything of a paranormal or religious nature. The milking-shed was near to the farmhouse which fronted part of the farmyard. The priest who had been called found the witness in a state of complete collapse, shaking with fear. His story was that he had been milking, had switched off the machinery, and, glancing down, saw a border-collie dog run down the centre gangway of the milking parlour. He realized it was a stranger and not one of his own dogs, but as it came nearer, he found he was seeing the far wall through the apparition. He was unable to describe how it vanished, as he was in such terror. The counsellor explained that common worries or stresses, or even increased psychic sensitivity or an altered state of consciousness on the part of one of the members of the family, could have caused a place memory to be activated. That explanation led to the client's revealing that there had been a recent upheaval in the family's life. The farmer was reassured and the phenomenon did not recur.

Case 10

A young family were awakened one night by what sounded like burglars. The father opened the bedroom door to find groups of people walking along the landing of the house and disappearing through the far wall. He removed his wife and children from the house and called the police. They arrived with a dog; the dog refused to enter the house. A young police officer went in and saw the same phenomena as had been described by the family. The groups of people were dressed in period costume and appeared to be carrying bundles and looking very sad. On investigation, it transpired that the family had suffered a cot death some three weeks previously. The house had been built over the site of an ancient plague pit. It would appear that the trauma of losing a young child had reactivated the place memory. What the family were seeing was a memory of people carrying their dead to the plague pit on that site. The place was blessed and the family received bereavement counselling.

Case 11

A priest was visiting a couple in a small cottage in his country parish. As he chatted with the couple, he said jokingly, 'No doubt there's a ghost around here.' Rather to his surprise, the wife said cheerfully, 'Oh, yes; we often see her.' Shortly after they had moved into the cottage, they saw the figure of a woman who appeared in a corner of the living room and proceeded to move diagonally up the wall. After several such 'sightings', they investigated the history of the house and discovered that at some stage the staircase had been moved to its present position from its original location, which was at the place where the apparition was seen. As the place memory or 'imprint' was spiritually and psychologically neutral and the people were not at all worried by it, there was no need for any kind of ministry.

Case 12

A priest was asked to visit an elderly lady who had lived for the last eighteen months in her newly-built old people's bungalow. She had seen quite distinctly a man in her bedroom, dressed in what appeared to be farm labourer's clothes of the nineteenth century. The room was small and she was on the side of the bed away from the man, whom she assumed at first to be a burglar. She said, 'I don't know who you are, but would you please go?' Although she was terrified, she was nevertheless wondering whether to try to defend herself with the stick she kept beside the bed. This proved to be unnecessary, as her visitor did in fact go away without harming her. She appeared, on questioning, to be intelligent and perfectly well-balanced, not under medication, with no history of neurosis, and no involvement with spiritualism or occult practices. Her bungalow was built on what used to be farmland, a few hundred yards away from the old farm, which had by then been demolished. No doubt that particular labourer had habitually used a path which had once passed by where the bungalows now stood. The counsellor was not able to tell the old lady why that particular labourer had left an 'imprint', or why she had picked it up. She had experienced no sense of any evil, and it did not seem as if the apparition was the result of past violence, crime or misdemeanour. Together with the old lady's daughter-in-law and a friend, the priest said prayers in the principal room, a special prayer in the bedroom for all those who had lived and worked on the farm in years gone by, and he blessed all the rooms and the garden. There was no further trouble.

Case 13

Over many years there had been very occasional reports by people alone in a particular church at night – for example, an organist practising – that they had seen someone moving behind them, 'out of the corner of their eye'. This they had felt to be a disturbing rather than a frightening experience. In one case the person concerned was able to tell the counsellor the whereabouts of what he had seen. The church itself had a very peaceful atmosphere. The counsellor asked two separate people who, he believed, had a gift of discernment in such matters, if they were aware of anything in the church, and they both independently chose the same spot, from which they claimed they felt some emanation coming up. This was roughly where 'something' had been seen. As the counsellor felt there was possibly a place memory at this spot, or possibly an earthbound spirit, he asked a priest to come and celebrate a requiem mass for the departed person – if such it was – with the church-warden and himself for congregation. Subsequently one of the people who had felt an 'emanation' revisited the church, and in the same place could feel nothing. There were no further reports of anything unusual, though the counsellor realizes that that in itself is not conclusive in any way. He has himself never been personally aware of anything out of the ordinary in that building.

The characteristic of the place memory is its repetitiveness. The phenomena may be audible or visible (occasionally both) but will have no relevance to what is going on at the present time. As the memory fades, the phenomena will have less and less meaning, and the clarity of what is perceived may become blurred and confused. At no time will the memory produce any physical effect, unless it has set off a poltergeist, or unless a poltergeist situation has revived and stimulated an old place memory. Stories of ancient 'ghosts' who have uttered dreadful warnings to the beholder should be dismissed as delusions or inventions, although occasionally there may be 'place previews' of a precognitive kind, as in the next case. Whether precognition is precognition of a predetermined future, or simply recognition of one of a series of possible futures such that the action of the person receiving the precognition may determine whether or not the event will turn out as precognized, is a moot point. Most people who believe in free-will prefer to hold the latter opinion.

Case 14

'Mike' was the fifteen-year-old son of a friend of the counsellor. He was a normal healthy schoolboy, although he had had an apparition of a man in grey near his home when he was about eight, and an out-of-body experience during a class lesson when he was fourteen. He left the counsellor's home, where he had been with his friend, in the early evening. He was on his cycle about half a mile away when a green car passed him, pulling into the middle of the road to do so. It was a narrow country lane and they were going uphill. Then, although it was dusk, the light seemed much brighter, and, to Mike's utter horror, the green car collided head-on with a red car coming downhill in the opposite direction. Mike, who was by now alongside the smashed red car, did not dismount but stopped, straddling the crossbar, his feet on the ground. He looked in at the driver's window and saw the driver and two passengers, all apparently dead, the driver crushed against the steering wheel. The whole vision was entirely vivid and 'real' yet he seemed to know it was a vision. He rode rapidly the remaining two miles home and told his parents. His father was sceptical but his mother rang the counsellor and he went immediately to see Mike. On close questioning, the counsellor assumed either a place memory (although he knew of no accident on that stretch within the previous seven years) or a precognition. Three weeks later, there *was* an accident at that point. A white van, waiting to cross the road, was run into by one of the other two cars which had collided on the main road. No one was killed, but three people were injured. Of the other two cars, one was red and the other green, but not (to the recollection of the counsellor) of the same make as the cars which Mike had 'seen'. No ministry of any kind was asked for or carried out, but the counsellor told the parents that if Mike should be troubled by further similar experiences, he would administer the laying-on of hands and would pray for that particular gift to be removed or directed by the Holy Spirit into useful channels.

There is another kind of 'place memory' (if it can be so called), produced by deliberate sin committed in the place concerned. Often this produces, not specific visual manifestations, but a lingering aura of unease and fear. The place may have been used for such purposes as prostitution, occult practices, or illegal abortions. Whereas the type of place memory so far discussed in this chapter seems to require a 'projector', the second type is more generally perceived, and often by persons otherwise not unduly perturbed by their emotions. A marked improvement in the pervading quality of the tone or mood of the place will be produced and noticed by all on the entry at the scene of a truly saintly person.

All readers will know of mysterious 'black spots' where accidents seem to cluster. Priests have been asked whether they can do anything to 'exorcize' such spots. Perhaps the first accident which occurred at this place has continued as a malignant place memory, so that a driver passing through the same place can become psychically attuned to the atmosphere of panic and dread and be so disturbed and off-guard as to cause another accident to happen. This, however, is only a suggestion. Much more documented research into 'black spots' is needed before any such theory could be considered proven. The counsellor may well feel that a 'black spot' of this sort can usefully be treated by the lesser exorcism of a place, as described in chapter 10 (page 90).

Pseudo-haunts

Just as there may be 'phoneygeists', so there may be 'pseudo-haunts'. They may be the result of fraud, or of misinterpretation of natural causes, or of mental disorder, or of hallucinations caused by the misuse of drugs or by post-hypnotic suggestions. Such hallucinations may be described in a way which loosely resembles a place memory, but they need to be dealt with by persons with a medical/psychiatric training and not by the amateur. Similar phenomena to those of a 'place memory' type may (according to some authorities) be caused by the creative imagination. According to C. G. Jung, there exist in the deep unconscious mind certain images to which he gave the name of 'archetypes'. These may differ in each race or culture, but are common to all members of each particular culture. It is possible that concentrated thought coupled with extreme exhaustion may release these archetypes and project them into visible form in the same way as the stresses which cause poltergeist activity result in physical movements. Because they are archetypes, these projected visions will always appear the same, and so be confused with the place memory described earlier in this chapter.

Fraudulent haunts are a different matter altogether. Trickery may be practised for a number of reasons – for the sake of notoriety; as a practical joke; for financial gain if it is desired to frighten a family into putting their house up for sale, or to obtain rehousing from a local authority; for publicity purposes if the premises are a hotel or public building. One member of a family may wish to frighten another; spiritualists, occultists, confidence tricksters, satanists, or other ill-disposed persons may wish to establish a reputation that a certain place is haunted, possibly to help preserve their own possession or use of it.

In such a case, the story presented to the counsellor will usually be very much too clear (and fit together with the reported phenomena too neatly) to resemble the mass of confused evidence which is usually presented in genuine cases. In the less intelligent cases of pseudo-haunt, the reported phenomena will go 'over the top' and contain obviously unreal aspects which have been culled from horror comics or films or television programmes, and which often reveal their inner inconsistencies when subject to even the mildest degree of cross-questioning. Descriptions of apparitions will almost certainly be provided and they will be well defined and go into great detail. 'Voices' will utter comprehensible messages. There will be a most unnatural order and tidiness about the whole haunt which the experienced counsellor will distrust at once. Extra suspicion will be engendered by the presence of the media at a place to which a counsellor has been called, as will the announcement by the reputed witnesses that they have no objection to publicity and, indeed, rather welcome it.

When this kind of pseudo-haunt is carefully fostered, and sedulously disseminated in the right places and to the right people, and especially if the media have given their attention to it, the whole situation may get completely out of hand. Many people may believe that they have personally observed the phenomena publicly described. Those outside the circle of the originator of the haunt may be fervent believers in the reality of the phenomena, and may contribute to the whole atmosphere of lurking dread. No amount of evidence of trickery can convince some people that all the reported events have a natural cause or are fictional accounts. The resulting atmosphere of horror and fear is just the kind of breeding-ground for genuine poltergeist phenomena, which add their own disturbances to the general upset which has been artificially created. If then some of the victims caught up in this scenario produce apparitions as a result of the psychic turmoil, the haunt may become almost a genuine one. By this time, any attempt to cool the atmosphere and replace panic by calm may be very hard indeed, and the counsellor may be forced to retire from the scene incapable of giving any practical help.

In other cases, a genuine haunt has died out and the phenomena have then been fraudulently repeated because the 'owner' of the 'ghost' has gained fame or notoriety, or has simply desired to convince sceptics of the authenticity of past phenomena. Tricks can be worked by children (even by very young ones) for the purpose of frightening or 'paying back' adults, for notoriety or to prolong the excitement caused by a haunt after the original phenomena have died out.

Some pseudo-haunts may arise simply because a suggestible person has misinterpreted normal events, and an atmosphere of dread has built up, in such a way that the most unsurprising of happenings is given a sinister interpretation. Counsellors should always be alert to this possibility. A few normal causes, either of mistaken reports of 'place memory' phenomena, or of disturbances misdiagnosed as poltergeist cases, are given here as a guide and suggestion:

1 *Structural*. Heat causing expansion or contraction of woodwork. Electric wiring faults. Draughts. Ill-fitting doors. Distortion of images which may arise when sunlight reaches a certain point through obscure glass.

2 *Environmental*. Shadows cast by street-lighting or passing car-lights. Noises in neighbouring properties. Noises carried along girders or heating or plumbing pipes. Rail or road noises or vibrations. Underground water. Ground subsidence.

3 *Animal*. Domestic animals or small pets. Rats, mice and large insects. Birds nesting in unexpected places such as disused chimneys.

Treatment of place memories

As with poltergeist disturbances, there is nothing in a place memory to be exorcized, so exorcism would be inappropriate and ineffective. Once the counsellor is satisfied of the genuineness of the events reported, his object should be to reduce panic and restore normality. If the phenomena are recurrent, he should try to establish the identity of the 'projector'. If there has been an emotional trauma which has precipitated the reactivation of the place memory, this will need to be pastorally ministered to. If the memories which are being reactivated are of past events only, and are not felt as threatening to the projector or reporters, the treatment may well be as follows:

1 Explain the nature and cause of the phenomena clearly and simply. Point out that, as they are memories, not entities, they are neither good nor evil. They have no volition and cannot forecast future happenings, nor can they communicate with living persons. They cannot harm the person who perceives them unless, by his own terror, he harms himself.

2 If the projector is consciously using psychic powers, he must be admonished to stop. If he is an occultist, he must renounce his practices immediately.

3 If the projector is unconscious of his powers, or cannot be traced, the only remedy is for the family to accept and establish some *modus vivendi* with the temporary difficulties until they wane or disappear completely.

4   If the projector can be identified, he should be blessed, and encouraged to make confession and receive sacramental absolution. It may well be that the trouble has been encouraged by personal anxieties or problems which may be resolved in this way.

5   The house and family should be blessed before the counsellor leaves, and arrangements made with the parish clergy for special oversight and encouragement to be given over a period of time. If the family are Christians and communicant, a Eucharist in the premises, with special intention for the peace of all who dwell there, and of those whose memories are causing the upset, is particularly appropriate. This could be a requiem Eucharist, or a Eucharist for the blessing of a house (see Appendix IV, pages 123 and 124) whichever seems best to fit the case. The importance of a special intention at any celebration of the Eucharist is not always realized.

6   If, however, the place memory falls into the special category of 'a cloud of sin' (see page 33 above), additional measures must be taken to improve the general way of life of the household concerned and its specifically Christian orientation. The inhabitants must be starkly presented with a choice. Either they go on living as they are, with the place memory growing blacker and blacker, or they abandon whatever practices are at the root of the reactivation of the place memory. If they choose the latter option, there will need to be an immediate and formal renunciation of the wrong practices, with confession and absolution. If the counsellor is part of a team, the senior team members will need to press this point privately upon each inhabitant in turn to inform all that they are in agreement as to the diagnosis and treatment, and then to administer sacramental absolution individually. There may then be a subsequent blessing (and aspersion with holy water, if appropriate) by the group as a whole. Explicit intercession should be made for the sinner(s) concerned, and prayer offered for them by all present. A supportive prayer group is especially beneficial. Religious houses can be a particular help in this respect. It is necessary to ensure that the parish priest concerned understands the necessity of the rapid integration of those involved into the Christian body in that parish, and of their long-term pastoral care and counselling.

5

The unquiet dead

Bereavement counsellors know that it is relatively common for a person who has recently lost a loved one by death to experience the hallucination of his continued presence. This may be expressed simply as a sense of his 'being there', but may also affect the sense perceptions so that the bereaved person feels the loved one's arm around his shoulder, hears his voice speaking words of comfort or guidance, smells the tobacco of his characteristic pipe, or even sees him walking in the street or sitting in his favourite armchair. The person who experiences this kind of thing may be puzzled by it, but is more often comforted than frightened. The most common explanation is that the bereavement is so intolerable that the unconscious mind refuses to believe that it has happened, and manufactures the phenomena in an attempt to convince the conscious mind that the loved one is still alive and present. Bereavement counsellors can deal with such cases as part of the whole pastoral process of helping a bereaved person adjust to his new situation.

Parapsychologists are familiar with the phenomenon of the 'crisis apparition' in which one person sees the figure of another person when that second person is not physically present, but is undergoing a great trauma or crisis in another part of the country, and, indeed, sometimes in another part of the world. The crisis may be a road accident, but is very frequently the crisis of death. The generally accepted explanation among parapsychologists is that such crisis apparitions do not involve the perception of a quasi-material 'ghost' or 'astral body' of the second person, but result from the first person receiving some sort of (telepathic?) message which is then exteriorized in apparitional form, sometimes at the very moment of the crisis, but sometimes delayed by a number of hours or even days.

Occasionally, however, neither of these two explanations of an apparition will be found to hold water, and the counsellor is forced to consider as a possible hypothesis that some particular and identifiable individual, though departed this world, is 'earthbound', and keeps troubling a person or a place with which during his life he had particularly strong emotional ties. The ghost of someone may be seen in the place where he lived or worked or died, and his appearance may be observed by independent witnesses who sometimes do not know him or the circumstances of his life and death until they make inquiries and discover them. In many cases the person whose ghost is seen will have died suddenly, tragically, or unexpectedly.

Apparitions of this sort seem to occur for one of three reasons:

1   The person whose spirit is seen may have been too much attached to the place he is haunting or the person to whom he is now appearing, and is loath to leave it. He may have lived only for that place or that person and may resent the making of new relationships which seem to exclude him from a bond which was previously exclusive to him. (The counsellor will also be wise to consider an alternative explanation, that is that the person perceiving the apparition is the one who feels guilt at the making of new relationships, and is unconsciously projecting a hallucination of the lost one as a means of exteriorizing this sense of guilt.) The guide to diagnosis of a case like this is to be found in the text, 'Where your treasure is, there will your heart be also' (Matt. 6.21). A building, a garden, a precious object, a certain person, could in any particular instance be classed as that 'treasure', the total affection, of the spirit while in this life, and the reason why the spirit cannot release itself from earthly ties.

2   The spirit may be in need of help and be calling for assistance in the only way it can attract attention. If so, the manifestations could, quite credibly, include the visible apparition and will certainly include a noticeable effect on the minds of persons in the immediate vicinity of the phenomena. If the spirit is in need of help, the manifestation will be pitiful. If, on the other hand, it is hostile, angry, or resentful, it will be an unpleasant ambience. If there is 'unfinished business' to which the spirit wishes to alert those to whom he is appearing, the feeling-tone will be appropriate (those who are familiar with the works of St Augustine of Hippo will remember his account, in *De cura pro mortuis* 11 (13), of the young man to whom his deceased father revealed the whereabouts of a missing receipt. They will also remember that Augustine characteristically and wisely cautions his readers against assuming too hastily that the source of the supernormal apprehension in such cases is necessarily the deceased person). In none of these cases will the apparition be dangerous to the percipient or the bystanders.

3   The spirit may be intent on giving comfort as best it can to a person whom it loved dearly and who is missing its physical presence. This last category will need to be discussed very sensitively indeed with the person who reports the sighting. It usually only lasts for as long as is really necessary for the spirit to convey reassurance and for the bereaved person to readjust to normalities of social involvement and activity. It is very hard in these cases to differentiate between what is 'in the mind' and what is an objective communication.

In the majority of instances caused by earthbound or unquiet spirits, the client will know, and will tell the counsellor, the name of the person whose spirit is causing the phenomena. Such haunts are more usually associated with a place than with a person, though they may pursue a client to various places if he was a near relative, spouse, or a very close friend with whom the departed person had a close and emotional attachment. Other haunts of this type are caused by spirits associated with the place but unknown to the client. They differ from 'place memory' haunts in that the apparition shows signs of intelligent volition and may react as though it can see the client, with whom it may appear to wish to communicate. As will be remembered, the place memory carries out an automatic and unintelligent ritual in apparently complete disregard of the presence of the perceiver.

While unquiet spirits do not themselves produce poltergeist phenomena, it may well be that mental stress on the part of those who are haunted can produce a small-scale attack of typical poltergeist activity.

Case 15

A family reported that they were seeing their recently-departed mother. She appeared in the house and was first seen by the father who saw her in his bedroom, and even saw her getting into bed with him. Appearances to other members of the family then followed. She had died in hospital; at the burial the coffin was found to be too big for the grave and became wedged while being lowered in. The family interpreted this as her reluctance to leave them, and the appearances were taken as confirmation of this diagnosis. Two local mediums visited the house at the family's invitation and confirmed this theory. When counselled, the family refused to use or hear the word 'cancer'; plainly they had never accepted that the mother's illness was terminal. The counsellor's eventual diagnosis was that the coffin's having become wedged was sheer accident, that the appearances really signified the family's unwillingness to say farewell to the mother rather than the mother's reluctance to leave them, and that the children's visions were caused by some kind of hysterical contagion after the father's initial experience. The family was given bereavement counselling and was advised to consider the phenomena, not as an 'unquiet spirit', but as the externalization of their own difficulties in coming to terms with bereavement.

Case 16

A suburban family described how they had been seeing a ghost in the upstairs part of their house. The mother, an artist, drew a picture of the ghost and some neighbours recognized it immediately as the picture of a former occupant, who had lived there some thirty years previously. Apparently at that time the house had been divided into flats. The woman who had lived in the upstairs flat had been in hospital to have her leg amputated. When she returned home, she discovered an eviction order and committed suicide. When the present occupants telephoned the immediately preceding occupant and asked her why she had moved from the house after only nine months' residence, they were told that it was because she had been seeing a ghost of a woman with one leg. A requiem mass was said in the bedroom. During the service the ghost appeared again, but went during the Prayer of Consecration. It has not been seen since.

Case 17

A woman complained that she was seeing individuals and clusters of people in historic dress. This had been going on for a year. At first she denied that anything of significance had happened to her during the preceding twelve months, but eventually she stated that her husband had died nine months earlier. She gave the day and the exact time that this had happened; clearly the death had made a profound impression. She and her husband had made a pact that whoever of them was the survivor would not mourn the loss of the other, because the other would still be present in spirit. The pact had proved impossible; one cannot legislate for the emotions of any other person, no matter how close and intimate. It then transpired that besides her husband's death, she had suffered the loss of a number of cousins within the previous eighteen months, and that one person had actually died in front of her late husband and herself. These incidents in turn evoked deep feelings about the deaths of her father and her two children. On closer questioning, it was found that the details of one member of her family corresponded closely with one of the apparitions. This unlocked a detailed comparison between the historical figures she had seen and various people in her life who had died in the previous eighteen months. These apparitions ceased after she had been given 'permission to grieve', and the house had been blessed and had had a requiem Eucharist celebrated in it.

How many of these cases are examples of the activity of the unquiet dead, and how many are subjective hallucinations caused by the traumas suffered by the person seeing them, is for the reader to decide. The same choice will confront the counsellor in very many cases of similar type. Again, whether the cure is successful because it actually does something for the unrested spirit, or whether it works because of the power of suggestion in colluding with misinterpretations put upon the phenomena by the person experiencing them, is a moot point. To some extent it does not matter so long as distress is relieved. If, however, the counsellor is prepared to accept the possibility of discarnate causes for cases of this type, and if he is convinced that this possibility is likely in a particular case, treatment is relatively easy.

The counsellor will recall that he is dealing with a human soul which needs salvation or guidance, and not with a demonic entity which could be commanded to 'depart to its own place'. Exorcism, therefore, would be a completely wrong form of treatment. The endeavour of the counsellor and his team will therefore be to introduce an atmosphere of love (and, where necessary, pity) for the departed spirit which needs to be ministered to. Gentleness and helpfulness are the guiding lines for any action, and the focus of attention should be directed to the suffering departed soul, not to the relief of the subjects of the haunt.

The object to be achieved is the direction of the soul away from its obsession with earthly matters into the mercy and the peace of Christ, thus replacing its present existence of unrest and disquiet with rest in eternity and light perpetual. The ritual actions are therefore straightforward, and are:

1   A requiem celebration of the Eucharist, performed on the site, with

special intention for that departed soul, with members of the family and friends of the departed taking a full and active part.

2   Explicit prayer for the repose of that spirit, offered at the time by all concerned, and continuing afterwards by members of the family or the inhabitants of the house where the disturbances have been taking place.

3   Bereavement counselling may well be appropriate; in any case, the importance of pastoral aftercare and of the adoption of the afflicted person into the body of Christian fellowship cannot be overstated.

4   The counsellor should help those involved to devise a few simple prayers for their continuing use, or write out a few simple prayers and leave them behind for their use and guidance.

6

The occult and the psychic

'Occult' means 'hidden', and the term is a portmanteau word for a wide variety of beliefs or practices which all have at their heart the conviction that there are hidden powers and forces in the universe which may be revealed to, or unlocked by, those who are 'in on' the secret. The search of the occultist is therefore a search for hidden knowledge which is denied to those outside his circle. This knowledge can, he believes, be used for good or ill, but his aim is to gain control and exercise power by the right manipulation of the objects of his knowledge. Occultism is therefore more akin to science than religion and its attitude to truth is essentially pragmatic and highly individualistic. God or the gods or the powers behind the universe are not worshipped; they are manipulated and used for purposes decided upon by the occultists. To the Christian, worship is primary, in that it is a means of aligning one's self with the will of God and submitting to it (in the joy of the service of him 'whose service is perfect freedom'). To the occultist, worship, if offered at all, is a means to an end, and there is a self-regarding aspect (or an aspect in which the gifts are far more important than the giver) to the whole business.

The 'psychic' is not the same as the occult, though there is in practice a great deal of overlap. The psychic is concerned with the potentialities and powers of man as a creature, or with the 'inner' side of nature seen as possessing some of the attributes of mind or of personality. Telepathy is part of the psychic, but by no means the only part. There are also the paranormal gifts of inner seeing and hearing, natural prophecy, hypnosis, dowsing – in short, a whole range of natural, intuitive abilities, not all of which are recognized by conventional science or psychology. What they have in common is that, despite appearances to the contrary, they are all part of the realm of nature and created by God. Like all created powers, the psychic needs to be 'hallowed and directed aright', but in itself it is as morally neutral as any other human ability – artistic or musical ability, scientific or financial expertise. Despite the popular selective quotation, money is not the root of all evil; it is 'the love of money' which is so described in 1 Timothy 6.10. So with the psychic. It is not evil in itself, but it can be misused by evil people for evil purposes, or used carelessly and without right thought so that it goes sour on the practitioner. All human abilities are powers, and care, prayer and control are required in the proper use of power. Otherwise, power will be used for less than the best purposes, despite good intentions.

The psychic and the spiritual are often treated as synonymous by those who know no better. The spiritual is concerned with the relationship of man to God, and is the inner side of man considered as a child of God by grace. The psychic is not in itself spiritual, though it may be used for spiritual purposes – again, like many of the intellectual or artistic gifts which God may give to certain individuals in greater or less measure. The 'mystical', again, is not to be confused with the occult (despite the definition of 'occult' given in the *Oxford English Dictionary*). Properly used, it refers to the direct and intuitive awareness of the divine through grace. It is unfortunately often used to refer to psychic intuition. This misuse of the term comes about through a confusion between the psychic and the spiritual. Natural, psychic intuitions are not necessarily bad, though they may be flawed (as any natural human propensity may be flawed by the effects of the Fall). The danger comes when people trust in them without subjecting them to critical scrutiny, and assume that because they are psychic they are beyond the need for questioning.

Magic, which is related both to the occult and to the psychic, is the attempted imposition of the will on circumstances or people. In its practice it uses occult mechanism or formulae or understandings in order to manipulate psychic power. It is a constant temptation – some Christians use prayer in a similar manner and need again and again to be recalled to the recollection that the attitude of prayer must always be 'thy will, not mine, be done'. To do otherwise is to fall into the temptation of 'ye shall be as gods'. While there are people who hold that it is possible to be a Christian occultist by using arcane knowledge in a wholly God-directed way, it is never possible to be a Christian magician. A Christian aims to serve God, while a magician seeks to wield power to his own will.

If we define magic as the attempt deliberately to manipulate psychic power in order to impose the magician's human will on circumstances or people, then if those intentions are good, it may be termed 'white magic' and if they are not, it is 'black magic'. Clearly there is harm in black magic, but it is not so easy to see the dangers in white magic, except for the sense of power which it may generate in the magician himself, or in the sense of dependence it may produce in those who believe that they are benefiting from the good that he is directing towards them. Nevertheless, magic is always sub-Christian, and God has forbidden us deliberately to engage in it. We are to seek, not our own will, but God's, and we are not to usurp God's place. All forms of manipulation of people are wrong. Psychic manipulation, whether by magical or by purely psychological methods (as in personality cults or in unscrupulous advertising techniques) is particularly dangerous and unethical, because it can be done so subtly that the people who are being manipulated can be unaware of what is being done to them.

There are occult organizations, to which we shall be referring in the next chapter, but a great deal of the occult use of psychic potentials is carried out in a completely unorganized way, especially as regards the use of ouija board and tarot cards. These can link up with spiritualistic or mediumistic practices, although spiritualism itself is more akin to a half-Christian heresy than to the occult as such. Organized spiritualism is a cult based on a somewhat credulous approach to highly selective aspects of paranormal phenomena. In seeking continuing contact with the dead, spiritualists may prevent those who have lost a loved one from carrying out the necessary work of bereavement, and this may have untoward psychological consequences. There is always the danger that spiritualists, in seeking guidance from the dead, may assume that the dead are necessarily wiser than the living. The best spiritualists are acutely aware of this danger, but the rank and file seem to be less cautious. Many spiritualists have a high and idealistic moral tone, and often see the dead as channels of communication for 'advanced souls' to give 'spiritual' teaching and guidance. Many of their messages reflect the genuine spiritual yearnings of mankind, expressed in a liberal sprinkling of contemporary popular (and especially Eastern or pseudo-Eastern) thought. For many of them, God is only an impersonal force in the background, and there is a tendency to play down the gravity of sin, the pervasiveness of evil and the need for atonement of sinful humans to a holy God. Jesus, therefore, if he is respected, is generally seen as a great prophet, a great teacher and, especially, a great medium (who, for example, conversed with Moses and Elijah on the Mount of the Transfiguration) and not as a Saviour and Lord.

Spiritualists are not so much evil and wrong as limited in their apprehension of spiritual truth. They will not be helped by condemnation, though it may often be necessary to point out the baleful effects of a too credulous reliance on their revelations as inspired or infallible. Some spiritualist claims are the result of accepting as genuine, phenomena which are in truth the result of coincidence, fraud, trickery or psychic manipulation, but there are others which accord with psychic reality, and this we must be prepared to acknowledge. We need, then, to go on from that point and show that the psychic is a part of nature, and that grace does not destroy but perfects nature by placing it in its true, that is God-centred, context. There must be at all times an emphasis on God as the great reality to which all human efforts and aspirations need to be directed, a teaching about the true nature of the communion of saints, eternal life and the gifts of the Spirit, and especially a proclamation of the gospel of Christ as mediator and atoner between God and man. The atonement is the great stumbling block in Christianity for very many spiritualists, and yet once the need for atonement is realized, nothing less than the full gospel will satisfy.

The Bible contains a number of warnings concerned with psychic phenomena (see, for example, Lev. 19.31; 20.6, 27; Deut. 18.10–11; Isa. 8.19–20). When these are considered in their context, certain permanent principles clearly emerge:

1   Loyalty to God and his perceived will must be paramount. We must take no action that would draw us away from him. Those called by God to study this area must always be on their guard against the danger (*not* the automatic consequence) of the stimulation of religious emotions which are afforded no adequate outlet and are therefore misdirected and become idolatrous. When that happens, the person is 'stuck on the psychic' and, spiritually, gets no further.

2   There is a permanent warning against the dangerous assumption that the dead are necessarily wiser than ourselves. Dependence on mediumistic guidance is a bar to all spiritual progress, and, in the spiritual life, one has to move forward or backward – there is no standing still. Modern spiritualists look for 'proof of survival'. This was not the concern of the ancient world which, by and large, took survival (in an extremely attenuated form) for granted.

3   Sorcery is forbidden. In the ancient world magical power was regarded as an inert force which could be activated by appropriate actions or incantations. To do this was regarded as utterly unlawful and a great danger to society (as we today would look upon a terrorist with atomic small-arms). Especially detested were the necromancers who were thought to be able to extort secrets from the dead and disturb their rest, frequently by revolting practices involving severed parts of corpses. Such

attempts belong entirely to the sphere of black magic. Mediums do not do this, but see themselves simply as offering channels for such of the dead as wish to speak through them. The use of the term 'necromancer' to describe a medium is incorrect and insulting. The 'witch' of Endor (so termed in the marginal headings of the King James Version of 1 Samuel 28, but not within the text) was not a medium but either a sorceress or wise-woman or a necromancer. Many modern translations of the Old Testament wrongly use the word 'medium' where a more accurate translation would be 'necromancer'. The idea of a witch being a person who has made a compact with the devil is one which does not belong to biblical religion but to medieval Christianity.

4   The biblical prohibitions, therefore, refer to an unauthorized and unspiritual manipulation of the psychic along the lines of the old, pre-Israelite, amoral nature worship. Such practices were forbidden because they involved a divided loyalty to the Lord, and therefore hampered people from developing along the lines God willed. In the psychic or occult sub-cultures of today's world, there are still people like this. Christians will want to release them from their bondage to the elements of the purely natural world into the liberty of the servants of God who can use the natural world in a spiritual way, in God's service and to God's glory.

The realm of the psychic, and psychic gifts, are neither holy nor demonic. There is no need to echo Kurt Koch's despairing dictum, 'the worst misfortune that can befall a Christian is the sudden acquisition of psychic gifts'. These gifts are natural, and the sudden realization of them may be unsettling, but a Christian with them has no need to despair. He will certainly need to exercise discrimination and discernment, and can benefit from wise spiritual counsel; but then, that should be true of all Christians who aim to grow in grace and exercise the gifts with which God has endowed them. Psychic gifts, like other gifts, should only be cultivated in relationship to God's will, and their exercise should be seen as a call to deeper commitment to God and a closer walk with him. If a person with such gifts finds that he cannot do this, and that he is getting things so out of proportion as to be unbalanced, then he should realize that the danger-signals are sounding and he should withdraw at once and totally. Just as a person who cannot control his alcohol intake has to eschew something which most people can use happily and in a responsible way, so some people cannot retain their balance in respect of psychic forces and have to forgo the use of them.

There are dangers in the psychic realm. Mediums can be fraudulent, or they can be genuinely mistaken. The messages they relay can be entirely self-generated expressions of wish fulfilment coming from the medium's own mind. They can be telepathic messages picked up from her sitters. Or they may be from discarnate sources, in which case they need to be very critically assessed before they are accepted and given credence. A person who lays herself open to any stray psychic influences (as a medium presumably must when she goes into trance and prepares to pass on messages from the 'beyond') may not always find herself becoming the mouthpiece of entirely good forces. Christians should be wary of any person who claims to be 'controlled' by any spirit other than the Holy Spirit of God, and they should constantly test the spirits to see whether they are wholesome or baneful. People who go to mediums at a time of bereavement are at particular risk. They invest a considerable amount of emotional capital in the exercise, so that their critical faculty is dormant. They can become addicted to receiving 'messages' from their loved ones via the medium, and rely upon them in order to maintain their emotional equilibrium. Most importantly, they can use the seances as a means of denying the death of the loved one, and so be unable to work through the natural and proper stages of bereavement to a mature and stable position.

Mediumship is often practised within the context of organized spiritualism, as divination is used within occult organizations; but the methods used by mediums and diviners may also be used entirely outside any psychic or occult organization. Casualties from amateur use of the ouija board or of tarot cards are unhappily frequent.

Ouija uses the letters of the alphabet, and standard responses such as 'yes' and 'no', either on a board or cut out and laid in a circle on a table. The board has a marker, or there may be an upturned wineglass on which all who are present place their fingers. The pointer or glass appears to move of its own volition and may spell out messages. It is possible that ouija 'works' either by psychokinesis or by unconscious energy transmitted through muscular activity on the part of the sitters. Whether this activity is powered by the sitters' subconscious or by directing spirits is a moot point. If it is the work of spirits, we have no means of telling whether they are well-meaning and truthful, or evil and intent on deceit. If it is the work of the subconscious, then the sitters take the messages literally as communications from an outside entity when they may be veiled and symbolic and arise from that part of the subconscious where repressed images, unacceptable to the conscious mind, are lurking. Such

49

images may well be of violence and death, and if taken literally may cause great fright and upset, and even lead to mental breakdown.

Tarot cards contain symbols, and are cut and shuffled to obtain answers to questions or problems. The reader, who needs to have studied the symbolism and meaning of the cards in some depth, uses the symbols and his knowledge (and/or psychic intuition) to indicate an answer or an insight into the situation, or as a form of 'fortune-telling'. The I Ching, or ancient Chinese 'Book of Changes', operates in a very similar way and its use is increasing in popularity at the present time. Books of guidance for the interpretation of tarot or I Ching symbolism are published with bewildering frequency.

The danger with tarot and I Ching is that the power of suggestion is greater than many people realize. The cards correspond to archetypal images deep within the unconscious mind, and they can set off powerful resonances which upset the subject's mental and emotional balance. The dabbler, wise in his own conceit, is more at risk than he realizes. He is not on his guard, nor has he sought the protection of Christ. Indeed, ouija is often tried out by the emotionally and spiritually immature in an atmosphere of dare-devilry, with the frisson of experimenting in an area which is known to be disapproved of by many people. The dabbler may well be on his way to bondage to occult powers before he knows what is happening to him. The only advice to offer him is, 'don't'.

Case 18

A group of long-distance lorry drivers were meeting at motorway stops and playing with a ouija board. Some of them then experienced 'spirits' in the cabs of their lorries, trying to force them off the road or into oncoming traffic. They then became very frightened and went to see a priest. He tried to explain what they had been doing in terms of psychological forces rather than spiritual ones. It became apparent that, while playing with the ouija board, various unresolved conflicts within their unconscious minds had been brought to the surface and they had been unable to cope with them. The problems presented themselves in the guise of 'spirits' intent on destroying them. The group were persuaded to make an act of renunciation, to destroy the ouija board and to meet the priest to talk out their experiences and their interpretation of them.

Case 19

A sixty-year-old widow was deeply distressed after the loss of her husband, and visited a local medium. The medium gave her messages from her husband and the widow become convinced that he was still alive and in contact. She visited the medium two or three times a week (paying £10 per visit) and appeared to have become very dependent on her. A year after her bereavement, she suffered a major mental breakdown which the psychiatrist regarded as the result of a delayed and distorted grief reaction. Her visits to the medium had prevented her from passing through the normal stages of grief.

Case 20

An eighteen-year-old girl started to visit an Indian fortune-teller each Friday after being paid her wages. Her palm-readings began at £5 per session and gradually increased until she was unable to pay any more. When asked to pay £50 for a reading, she told the fortune-teller that she could not afford to come and see him again. On hearing this news, he muttered under his breath that her palm indicated that she was going to die soon. The girl became very frightened. Soon she was not sleeping or eating and her health was rapidly deteriorating. She then saw a priest who tried to show her that she was very suggestible; she had nothing to fear, but had been the victim of an unscrupulous clairvoyant. The girl was referred to a psychotherapist who used the hypnotic technique of counter-suggestion as a means of persuading her that she was not going to die.

Occultism covers a very wide field, impossible to detail in all aspects. It is not 'religion', not even 'false religion', but fringe science or alternative science. The true occultist is not worshipping anything (not even Satan) but is trying to use secret powers to his own advantage. Some Satanists, however, in reaction against Christianity, have invented a pseudo-worship of Satan in which they use an inversion of the Eucharist, known (by others, not by them) as the 'Black Mass'. More often, occultists will be amoral about evil, seeing it as a necessary counterbalance to good rather than something to be fought against and extirpated. But it should be emphasized that 'the occult' covers a mass of beliefs and practices, lacking rigid dividing lines of dogma, and fluid and kaleidoscopic in organization. In the following chapter, we attempt a brief historical construction of the origin and rise of occultism, Satanism and witchcraft, try to show how converts to these beliefs may be won, and indicate some lines along which Christians may act if they meet followers (or ex-followers) of these beliefs who want to break free from them but find it is hard to escape.

7

Occultism, witchcraft and Satanism; sects and cults

Many of the groups of the kind we shall be considering in this chapter operate in considerable secrecy, so that knowledge of them has to be built up piecemeal by the careful collection of information. Many of these groups split or amalgamate, form, re-form, and go out of existence with bewildering rapidity, and their membership tends to fluctuate, so that any detailed picture which could be given at any one time would become out of date very quickly. For that reason, the present account will confine itself to generalities.

The Christian Exorcism Study Group, however, likes to be able to give as much information as is possible to any bona fide counsellor who needs to know the nature and connections of an organization with which a client may have become involved. Any priest or congregation who discovers the activity of a witchcraft, Satanist or occultist group is therefore asked to pass on to the Group any information he has. Much of what follows in this chapter has been condensed from extensive material in the possession of one member of the Group who has made a special study of this field.

People become involved in these sort of groups for a whole variety of reasons and in a whole variety of ways. They may only penetrate as far as the relatively innocuous fringe, or they may become involved at a very deep and serious level. Some groups are more pathetic than dangerous, and simply serve to bolster the self-esteem of the lonely or insecure. Ways into involvement are manifold:

1   In Britain, it was the repeal in 1951 of the Witchcraft Act, which had been on the statute book since 1735, which enabled occultists and others to pursue their beliefs, practices and recruitment relatively untrammelled by fear of prosecution. The liberalizing of society since then has assisted in this process, and there is now an increasing number of occult books, magazines and shops from which information may be gleaned, so that a large proportion of the population is currently aware of the subject. It

must be stressed, however, that even today not all the practices of all occult and Satanist groups are within the law. This British revival of occultism is part of a worldwide phenomenon, affecting Europe and North America in particular.

2   Articles about the subject appear from time to time in the local or national press. The subject has been introduced by some secondary schools into the Religious Studies curriculum of children in their earliest teens. Some people, on hearing of this area of knowledge or seeing books about it, are intrigued by a sense of the mysterious, or catch for the first time a glimpse of their own intuitive nature. In all innocence they may be 'taken in' and pursue the matter in their own way, until picked up by a serious practitioner.

3   A number of universities and polytechnics contain a few people who form unofficial occult, witchcraft and/or Satanist societies. They will rarely call themselves by these names, as they will wish to cover up their true nature, but they function to recruit the academically brighter members of the community.

4   Some members of occultist groups are known to frequent coffee bars and the sort of establishments popular with youngsters in their middle teens. These groups tend to have a more insecure membership, and are simply looking for schoolchildren in order to boost their numbers, their finances and their sense of self-importance.

5   Adult recruits may be picked up in public houses, often in 'singles bars' as unattached men or women. Drinks are bought for them and they may be invited to a party while the worse for alcohol. The party may become more intense or reveal its serious side, at which stage the potential initiate may realize he cannot withdraw without the risk of exposing himself to blackmail. The people most likely to be trapped into a movement in this way are the young, the sexually deviant, the lonely, and unscrupulous entrepreneurs who see opportunities for gain within this particular sub-culture.

6   Satanist groups may find there is financial reward to be had from activities such as drugs-trafficking or blackmail. People with a criminal tendency may become involved either because they think there is money in it, or because they see the chance of establishing power over others, or as a way of social advancement. Others may seek success in business or politics through contacts gained by membership of such groups.

7   Before long, anyone who shows interest in the occult will meet someone else who is more involved. As occult secret societies are 'wheels within wheels', thus will begin the long process of deeper and deeper involvement. Outer groups of various kinds exist, perhaps practising some form of spiritism, astrology, palmistry, transcendental meditation, tantric yoga or theosophy. It is rare for such groups to be purely 'front organizations' for anything more serious, but very often there will be people who use their membership of 'soft' groups in order to recruit members for 'harder' occultism.

8   There is a process of advancement whereby selected members of an occultist group can be invited to join something of a 'higher grade' in which they are promised that further secrets will be revealed. Inner occultist circles are very particular in their choice of recruit. Interested persons are carefully vetted and undergo close scrutiny before they are allowed to pass the threshold. For example, witchcraft in itself is relatively harmless, and most witches will profess (rightly or wrongly) to be 'white' rather than 'black' practitioners; but Satanists regard covens as possible nurseries for their cult, and may even take over whole groups, so that their members will then be sucked into Satanic activities by way of their involvement in witchcraft or ritual magic.

Although these secret or semi-secret groups share common features, and although there may be links between some of them, and a degree of shared membership, in fact occultism, Satanism and witchcraft are not the same. They differ in their underlying philosophy and ethos and need to be distinguished. We will attempt the kind of broad description which enables this differentiation to be achieved, without going into the kind of detail which could soon become out of date and misleading. Since some religious and quasi-religious cults share some methods of recruitment with these groups, and since the process of deliverance from them has aspects in common, we will also add a note about cult involvement and rescue.

Occultism

Occultists believe they are in possession of ancient and arcane knowledge about the nature and workings of the world. The different groups vary in the source they claim for this secret knowledge, but they all, in effect, seek salvation through the possession and understanding of divinely revealed knowledge, whereas the Old Testament saw salvation as coming through the Covenant initiated by Jehovah, and the New Testament sees it as given by God's grace to those who put their faith in the atonement wrought through the death of Jesus.

Almost all occult groups currently active date from the nineteenth or twentieth centuries, though nearly all of them will claim a descent from very much older groups, and their manuals are of considerable antiquity. Some base themselves on the Hermetic writings, some on the Qabala, some on Rosicrucian material. Many are extremely eclectic and syncretistic, and new systems and interpretations are constantly being published, so that to some extent one thinks of the occultists as like the Athenians of St Paul's time who 'spent their time in nothing except telling or hearing something new' (Acts 17.21).

The *Corpus Hermeticum* is the name given to a collection of up to twenty Greek and Latin writings (the enumeration varies) containing religious or philosophical teachings ascribed to Hermes Trismegistus. A second collection, also ascribed to the same author, contains a mass of astrological, alchemical, magical and similar material. Hermes is the Greek name of the Egyptian god Thoth, the father and protector of all knowledge. The Hermetic writings probably date from the first to the third centuries AD, and their mystic teaching has as its aim the deification of the adept through the proper knowledge of God. Links with neo-Platonism are strong.

When the Roman Empire accepted Christianity as its official religion in the fourth century, the pagan mystery schools were suppressed and had to work secretly under cover of such sects as the Manichees and Paulician gnostics. Secrecy because of the persecution of 'heretics' reinforced the claim that such sects were the trustees and inheritors of ancient secret knowledge which alone secured full salvation, and that 'ordinary' Christians had only a publicly-known system of very limited power. Between the fourth and twelfth centuries, these dualistic sects spread westwards and influenced movements which became known by various names – Bogomils in Bulgaria, Cathars in Germany, Albigensians in southern France. All of these feed to some degree into the lore of present-day occultist groups, though, again, they are used very selectively and there is no continuous historical link, only a picking-up of ideas after an interval of many centuries.

The Qabala (Kaballa, Caballa, etc) is a heterodox Jewish system borrowed from Aramean Chaldeans in Babylonia which was first brought to Europe by Aaron ben Samuel in the ninth Christian century, and flourished in Troyes from about 1070, where it became influential in the rise of the Knights Templar *c.* 1114. After the suppression of the Templars, the movement flourished underground for some time. Most modern occultist groups claim succession of their tradition from the Templars. The Qabala includes a deal of numerological exegesis of the Hebrew text of the Old Testament, which reveals hidden doctrines to its initiates. God is held to emanate creation through ten successive stages, the final one of which is the world we live in. Some of his emanations were mistakes, and he appointed a special angel to conceal this fact from man.

The founder of Rosicrucianism, the original 'Christian Rosicross', was a certain Christian von Reogsen who journeyed in the Middle East in the early thirteenth century, met Templars, Druzes and some unorthodox Sufis and members of other occult bodies at various points in his travels, and produced a syncretistic system of beliefs out of them all.

The continuing links between any of these bodies so far mentioned and modern occultism are tenuous and some of them may even be fanciful, but they figure largely in the legitimation of occult lore. Occultist bodies tend to form and re-form in varying combinations, and the scene is a remarkably fluid one. When one moves from purely philosophical occultism to its practical and ritual aspect, one is beginning to overlap greatly with the sphere of magic. A magician is someone who uses his hidden knowledge to affect the outside world of things or the inner disposition of persons. There can be occultist magicians, pagans, witches and Satanists, all believing in magic as a way of giving practical effect to their beliefs. If Christians are accused of doing the same through their prayers and rituals, they must remember that the essence of Christian prayer is the alignment of the praying soul with the will of God, whereas the essence of magic is the attempt to bend the forces of the universe to the will of the magician.

Witchcraft

No one knows the origins of present-day English witchcraft. Groups could be the survivors of original Celtic paganism which took over the sites and religion of the Stone Circle cult in prehistoric times. Stonehenge and Glastonbury are sacred places to many witches and occultists. They claim that 'ley-lines' exist: lines of psychic influence activated by magic rituals and linking places of particular psychic significance by straight lines, often over considerable distances. There may well be a system of ley-lines focusing on Glastonbury and Stonehenge, as well as other systems elsewhere in the country. Some psychic sensitives claim to be able to tell from a kind of inner 'buzz' when they are crossing one of these lines. Since they link ancient sites, and many Christian churches were built on the site of earlier pagan worship, some witchcraft and occultist groups may try to use Christian churches in which to hold their own rituals unknown to the present priest or his congregation. If they are frustrated in this, they will use stone circles and ley-lines where they are not on sites now Christianized, but whether this is anything more on their part than unhistorical romanticisim about the ancient Celtic religion is doubtful.

A second theory as to the origin of witchcraft relates it to the influence of heterodox Muslim mystics (Sufis) from North Africa and Spain during the early Middle Ages, with a double-horned moon cult.

Much the most likely, however, is that (apart from examples of the survival of ancient paganism in isolated village communities) present-day English witchcraft dates back no further than the early twentieth-century occult revival. It is a development from paganism and is akin to a form of nature-worship. 'White' witches are those who claim to use the forces of nature for a beneficial purpose; 'black' ones are those who seek to employ them in a malign way, to cause harm to their enemies or to the enemies of their clients. Witches often claim to be the successors of the ancient Druids, but so little is really known of the Druids that the link is probably fanciful.

Pagans in modern Britain may be divided into those who worship masculine and those who worship feminine deities. The 'masculine'-oriented pagans often worship the 'Life-force' and reject Christianity with what they (following Nietzsche) call its 'slave morality'. Their favourite gods are the Norse deities and one of their magazines was called the *Raven Banner*. The 'goddess worshippers', on the other hand, are particularly concerned with creativity, intuition, compassion, beauty and co-operation. They see Nature as the outward and visible expression of the divine, through which the goddess may be contacted. They have therefore more to do with ecology and conservationism than with orgies, and are often gentle worshippers of the good in nature. They, too, may claim a link with the ancient Druids, though again this is fanciful and unhistorical.

Witchcraft is also, basically, worship of (or manipulation of) the forces of nature. The male and female principles in nature are represented by a horned god and a moon goddess. There is little or nothing, however, in common between witchcraft as persecuted in the Middle Ages and the early modern period, and the coven witchcraft which is practised today. Nudity, for example, is never mentioned in the historic witch trials and that and flagellation seem to be modern inventions which give witchcraft an appeal to those whose sexual fantasies have not progressed far beyond an adolescent phase.

Coven witchcraft is on the increase. There is little evidence of great organization, and groups seem to be independent of each other and to choose their beliefs and rituals according to the reading and ideas of their leaders. There is a deal of half-understood theosophy and Eastern thought mixed up with pagan or occultist ideas and anthropological speculation in many magic practitioners or witchcraft covens. Since witches believe in the forces of nature, their festivals will be linked with the movements of the sun and moon, particularly with the solstices and equinoxes (25 March, 21 June, 29 September and 21 December) and with the full phase of the moon.

Witchcraft may be underestimated by Christians on the grounds that it is phoney and synthetic, and that its covens are completely eclectic and (unlike organized Satanism) belong to no national organization. There are, however, dangers. The whole of this area of behaviour is far from the concerns of true religion, which places its worshippers at the service of God rather than using the powers of the divine within nature to serve the needs and desires of humans. The more prurient aspects of coven behaviour may attract the immature, who see the whole thing as a way of combining a sexual 'kick' with the frisson of taking part in a forbidden activity, or one of which normal society would disapprove. The elaborate rituals in magic and witchcraft are valued, not as effective formulae which need to be voiced correctly if the spell is to work, but as methods of concentrating the will. Their power is therefore linked with the power for good or ill of the concentrated will. That psychic power may well be considerable, and the thought of it tempts some people to use witchcraft or magic for destructive purposes, and to become 'black magicians' rather than 'white witches'.

A belief in the possibility and efficacy of cursing as well as of blessing is widespread, and is known in many different cultures. Students of the Old Testament will recall the story of Balaam who was hired to pronounce a curse on the Israelites, but found himself unable to say anything other than a blessing (Num. 22–3). The thought that one may have become the victim of a curse still arises from time to time, and not only among ethnic minority groups. The exercise of discernment in such cases can be very difficult, and the Christian minister has to be careful to keep an open mind. West Indians, whether Christian or not, and Asian Muslims have occasionally sought some kind of ministry from a Christian priest to counteract the effects of a curse – effects which may range from business misfortune to actual illness. It is often not easy to know whether this is because a curse has been laid on the person concerned, or whether it is because the sufferer *believes* that a curse has been laid upon him. Loss of confidence is not unconnected with business misfortune, and the power of psychosomatic features in illness is well known.

When a series of calamities afflicts an individual or a family, or if an illness persists for which there appears to be no cause and perhaps no medical diagnosis, the possibility of the malign influence of a curse should not be ruled out. For instance, a case was brought to the attention of the Christian Exorcism Study Group of a person seeking the Christian ministry of healing for a mysterious malady of unknown origin. On questioning, it was discovered that the trouble started following a malediction spoken by a gypsy who had been refused some request months previously.

Case 21

A man in his fifties was made redundant with little hope of finding employment again. He saw this as the final blow in a series of unhappy events. He traced his personal problems, anxieties and accidents to a time when he believed he had had a curse put upon him. He went to a priest to ask for the curse to be removed. The moment of cursing, as he described it, happened one cold and wet January evening. He had travelled by train to a small town and arrived late in the evening. He was the only person to get off the train and the station was deserted. As he walked out of the station to find a taxi, he saw what he believed to be a ghost walking past him in the other direction. The ghost was tall and wore a brown cloak and hood and sandals. He believed that from that moment he had been cursed and that his life had gone wrong from then onward. The priest asked where the railway station in question was, and realized it was near a Franciscan friary. The 'ghost' was almost certainly one of the friars who had pulled his cowl over his head because it was raining. This interpretation was put to the client, who was then helped to look at his life in a more positive and thankful way. With this assurance he was able to get away from the sense of being under a curse, and to face the future with more confidence.

The Christian minister called in to help in an alleged case of cursing may want to be clear in his own mind whether curses have any objective power or reality, or whether they act entirely through psychological means. He may find himself believing in the possibility of telepathic or psychokinetic influences being transmitted from a distant sorcerer, or may find such an explanation entirely incredible. In the latter case, he will have to ask himself whether he ought to collude with what he takes to be the false beliefs of the sufferer in order to effect a cure by the same kind of psychogenic means as caused the illness, or whether he must maintain his own intellectual honesty and refuse to attempt a cure within the mental framework in which his client has understood his illness. It is often more helpful (and honest) to profess an open-minded agnosticism on the point, and to offer help along the lines of, 'I don't know whether this has been caused by a curse or whether there is some other explanation for it; but in either case the healing power of Jesus is going to be able to cope with it'. A ministry of prayer, with or without the laying-on of hands and/or anointing, will always be appropriate. What should be avoided at all costs is an attempt to provide some kind of Christian 'white magic' in opposition to an alleged evil force. Emphasize the healing power of Christ in a positive manner rather than the 'double negative' of Jesus as the person who destroys and neutralizes the forces of evil. It is the province of Christian ministry to spread calm and peace in the name of Christ in situations where fear prevails.

Finally, in this section on witchcraft, brief mention must be made of 'green witches'. These still remain in some isolated country areas. They are loners, certainly not banded together in covens, and their lore is handed on from generation to generation. They, and the hereditary witches, are probably dying out and will not often come to public notice.

Satanism

Satanism came greatly to public notice in 1986 during the trial at Maidstone Crown Court of Derry Knight, who was convicted on charges of obtaining over £200,000 by false pretences from a number of Christians who had been convinced that he required the money in order to buy Satanic regalia and to destroy a Satanic organization from within.

Opinions will differ as to whether Knight was simply a confidence trickster with an outsider's knowledge of the organizations he spoke about, or whether he really was well within Satanism and privy to many of its secrets; but in his summing-up after thirty-four days of court proceedings (as reported in *The Times* on 24 April 1986), Judge Neil Denison said to the jury: 'I suggest that you approach your assessment of the evidence against the background that Satanism does exist, and there can be no doubt that those that practise it are evil, depraved and dangerous.'

Witchcraft is essentially a pre-Christian understanding of the supernatural behind the forces of nature, but Satanists take up an explicitly anti-Christian position. They hold that the Creator God has withdrawn from his world and never intervenes in its affairs. The Son of God who has been given control of the earth in the Creator's absence is Satan, the 'god of this world' (see 2 Cor. 4.4). Jesus tries to wreck Satan's plan for the world, but Satan, they believe, will win in the end.

The sacred days of Satanism are therefore the nights of the new moon, when no reflected light from the sun can reach the earth, and on the nights of 1 February, 30 April, 1 August and 31 October. Those are the days when, at the latitude of Rhodes, Sirius is behind the sun when it rises or sets, reaches its highest point in the sky, or is at its lowest declination under the horizon. The great mystery of Satanism is symbolized by Sirius, the sun behind the sun. It is no coincidence that the feasts of Imbolc, Beltane (Walpurgis Night), 1 August and Samhain are the eves of the Christian feasts of Candlemas, St Philip and St James, Lammas and Hallowmass (All Saints), because the Christians have taken the older festivals over. For Satanists, Beltane and Samhain are the major occasions for the celebration of the Black Mass, when there may be gatherings of several hundred people from distant locations.

Progression within Satanism is finely graded by a series of initiations, and discipline between senior and junior is absolute. Major serious Satanist groups have international links, and seek to wield political and financial power. Some groups try to get their more influential members launched on a political or business career, though this is considerably more difficult than persuading people already involved in politics or finance to join 'circles'. The rituals of initiation are often sexually compromising, and may be photographed, so that if the initiate is tempted to leave the group, the utmost pressure (to the extent of blackmail if necessary) can be used to prevent this happening. Satanists are at work in some of the more extreme forms of left-wing or right-wing political activity. As has already been stated, the Christian Exorcism Study Group attempts to monitor the existence and activities of such organizations and groups and to ascertain the links between them.

The majority of Satanists not only hate and despise the Church, they may also fear it – though they would not like openly to admit this. They may break into churches to hold their rites or to desecrate the buildings by the scrawling of pentagrams on the altar or in other ways. In 1984, for example, three cases of this were reported within London. They like to corrupt the Church and its sacraments, and may attend the Christian Eucharist in order to obtain consecrated wafers. If they can procure a validly ordained clergyman who has renounced his Christianity, and have him celebrate their Black Mass, they see him as having a particularly high value in the war of Satan against the Creator God. If a member of the clergy can be corrupted and encouraged to join a black circle, he will be lavishly attended to and considered a prize catch.

The magical training practised by occultists or Satanists will include such activities as the fostering of powers of extra-sensory perception, astral or out-of-body travel, psychokinesis and levitation. They also undergo a form of group hypnosis which enables them to imagine the disappearance of the physical world and the summoning of demons to appear before them.

Psychic projection (not the same as psychological projection, which has already been mentioned on page 27, and will be more fully discussed on pages 71–2 below) is a phenomenon associated with magic or occultist practice which is particularly disturbing to the victim. It seems that some occultists are able to project ideas from their own minds to the minds of victims, who see them as forms apparently external to themselves. It is as if there is a kind of 'hypnosis at a distance' whereby the hypnotizer is not physically present, but influences the mind of his subject through extra-sensory means. What the subject 'sees', therefore, has no more objective reality than a vision caused by hypnosis; but it is a means of establishing control by the magician over his victim, who does not realize that there is no objective counterpart to what he imagines himself seeing. Such projections do not seem to be possible unless the magician has previously had personal contact with the victim, to establish sufficient rapport to make the projection work.

The manifestations will usually take the form of an apparition designed to cause the 'haunted' person to take some specific action. They may be of a fearful aspect and be designed to frighten the victim away from some particular place. Conversely, they could be seductive, and

63

designed to attract him away from some place or to surrender his will to that of the projector. In some cases, which are even more akin to post-hypnotic suggestion, there may be no actual visible apparition, but simply an irresistible feeling – an unaccountable dislike of, or even a positive fear of, some particular place. Or the victim may hear authoritative commands to do some special action, or he may feel impelled to do so for no particular reason. Alternatively, he may feel that he is being ordered to leave something or to abandon some course of action on which he has already embarked, feeling an indefinable sense of doom which lifts as soon as he changes course.

Projections which become visible seem to happen more often on ancient sites, or at least in the open air, than they do indoors. They may be in the nature of psychic 'scarecrows' protecting the site from intrusion. Although in themselves they have no objective reality, they may, if the site is being used for occult or Satanic purposes, acquire a type of low grade semi-independent life of their own and become demonic, malignant or dangerous. All projections, however, are to be treated as attempts to impose the will of one person or group upon another without the victim's conscious knowledge, and need to be counteracted.

When faced with evidence of projections, the counsellor should not attempt to exorcize unless there are additional demonic overtones, for example in a case where a member of a Satanist group is being attacked because he has left the group. In general, treatment should be based on the hypothesis that some ill-intentioned human being is attempting to use paranormal powers to force his will on some other person in a quasi-hypnotic way. Points to stress when counselling the victims of such attacks include the following:

1   The whole place should be blessed, and sprinkled with holy water.

2   All concerned in the case should be counselled to make a determined endeavour to live a life in harmony with one another, and to exhibit as much Christian faith as has been vouchsafed them.

3   Christian symbols, such as the crucifix or a holy picture or statue, may be used, to fix the attention and help the faith of those under attack.

4   When attacked,
    (i)   keep the mind calm, and remember that the projections have no independent reality;

(ii)   pray for help and call on the name of Christ, possibly grasping the Christian symbol for reassurance;

(iii)   stare at the projection, no matter how terrible it is, until the real surroundings can be seen through it and it completely fades.

5   There should be Christian intercession for the projector. Prayer should be directed to God *for* him, not against him or them. It should be realized that the Christian welfare of the projector needs to be forwarded, and that when this happens there will be a diminution of his occult powers.

6   Where it is suggested that the projection may be the result of post-hypnotic suggestion on the part of the projector, the employment of hypnotism as a means of removing the implanted will may be useful. This should not be attempted without medical advice and supervision.

Case 22

The Christian daughter of a clergyman, with no previous history of psychiatric illness or a vivid fantasy life, while at University made critical verbal attacks on the Satanist student society. For some weeks after this, she would be awakened during the night, and claimed to see transparent three-dimensional images of members of this group, who intimidated her in her locked bedroom. When questioned later, the members of the group admitted that they had met together, and concentrated on imprinting telepathically into her mind a mental projection of these images. After the concerted prayer of a number of Christians and the practice of 'St Patrick's Breastplate' by the Christian girl, the nocturnal attacks ceased.

Case 23

A large inner-city vicarage was occupied by an unmarried priest who let out various rooms as 'bed-sits' for students. A new vicar moved into the house and felt that one of the rooms appeared to be very cold and to have a 'strange feeling'. Various members of his family and visitors who had used this room said that they suffered from nightmares and were very unhappy about occupying it. The vicarage family contacted the former incumbent, who told them he had had to ask the student who used that room to leave because the other students were complaining that he was involved with black magic and using the room to carry out Satanist rites. The room was exorcized and blessed, and a Eucharist was celebrated there. After this, members of the family and visitors were able to use the room without ill effect.

Case 24

A middle-class family living in a London surburb had become involved in 'wife-swopping' parties. This led to their meeting members of a magical group. They went to meetings and were soon initiated, by which time they realized the group was Satanist in nature. Initially, only the husband and his wife were members, but they were also encouraged to make their eighteen-year-old daughter a member as well. When they realized how deeply they were involved, they wanted to leave, but were frightened of retribution and threats. Eventually the husband resigned his job and the family moved to another part of the country where they changed their name and began a new life.

Sects and cults

Lonely and vulnerable people may be ensnared by occultists, magicians and Satanists. They are also often considered 'fair play' by a number of religious or quasi-religious cults. There is frequently enough in common between the methods used to make converts to a cult and the methods used by some of the groups we have so far been considering in this chapter to make it worth while to include here a section on cults and their methods of proselytism. In general, their characteristics are fivefold:

1   The ruling power is held by a living and wealthy leader.

2   They are held together by a hierarchy of subordinate leaders requiring unquestioning obedience.

3   The system of belief is absolute and no other system is tolerated. The cults then consider themselves above secular law.

4   Individual rights are considered as of no importance. Intellect and achievement are scorned. All intimacy is controlled. There is thus devaluation of the self, and encouragement to achieve the goals established in the sacred doctrines of the cult. Scapegoats may be led to suicide. Murder in the name of the cult is not unknown.

5   The work of the group is money-collecting and proselytization.

The leaders claim special, unique, magical powers and responsibilities. They allow themselves to be considered prophets or messiahs. They have a unique world-view with an intense wish for power and a talent for influencing others. It may not be necessary for a leader to believe in his own doctrines, but it is likely that the sense of power over others gained from sudden conversions eventually will convert the leader himself, thus increasing his own sense of inviolability and omnipotence.

Thus stated, the nature of the cult seems obvious and its beliefs and practices unattractive. Yet it makes converts, who pursue the aims of the organization with frightening intensity. How does this come about?

1   Cult members are taught to spot a young student, arriving with knapsack and guitar at college. Such a person is often hungry at least, and often uncertain as to what his life at college is going to be like, and whether he will be able to find and keep friends. It is more than likely that he is passing through some life crisis.

2   The student is befriended, invited to investigate a rather simple proposition like 'love', and brought into the next stage of the conversion process. The general welcoming friendliness of all the cult members impresses him, and their ideals are often shared by the convert.

3   The next stage is characterized by deliberate, blatant deceit and distortion of reality. There is group pressure, endless lectures, singing, chanting and a constant barrage of rhetoric which captures the young idealist mind. This leads to a state of narrowed attention, with high suggestibility.

4   This new state of mind is akin to trance or dissociation. The subject has yielded up his uncomfortable autonomy and placed his body and mind in the hands of the group. Their persuasion of him has been in effect coercive, but he does not realize this, imagining that he has surrendered willingly, in the cause of ideals he believes in.

5   In this state of passive, narrowed attention and willingness to be influenced, conversion begins in earnest. This is characterized by unbelievable intensity, away from familiar surroundings, aided by change of diet. Indoctrination proceeds apace. Elements of guilt, terror and supernatural pressures are introduced. Promises of redemption, safety and rewards are made to the believer.

6   All activities are now done in a group. A stereotyped pattern of

67

behaviour is encouraged, and all familiar and loved past objects such as parents, brothers and sisters, home and home town, are seen in a different light so that as far as the convert is concerned they are of no significance and have almost no real existence. 'Reality' becomes narrowed down to present experience and present companions, and includes elements of the supernatural, the magical and the terrifying. Language is quickly and deliberately changed, and all words with emotional importance such as 'love' and 'family' are subtly altered in meaning so as to refer only to the cult and its members. Group tasks are given for the individual to learn, and soon it is as if the past never existed. The person is now dependent on the absolute authority of the cult, and all other thoughts and aspirations are obliterated from his mind.

7   This stage of major dissociation is now relatively simple to maintain, and is assisted by continued intensive chanting and procedures of meditation.

Escaping

The remainder of this chapter deals with the process of helping those who wish to escape from non-Christian or anti-Christian groups to do so. Where the will has been so manipulated that there is no desire to leave the group, it is a specialist business to track down the convert, and even more difficult to make personal contact and to break the 'spell' which is binding him to it. Counsellors asked by worried parents and relatives to help in this process may find that their diocesan bishop is in touch with experts and organizations with the necessary knowledge and experience.

If a person has belonged to a Satanist group and wishes to abandon it, it will not be easy for him, and he will need both practical and spiritual help from Christians. Involvement with Satanism means that one has been entrusted with the group's secrets. Men love darkness rather than light, because their deeds are evil (John 3.19). Christians are exhorted not to be involved in the deeds of darkness, but rather to reprove them and bring them to the light (Eph. 5.11). The really important secrets of a Satanist group are only known to the most senior members of its hierarchy, the so-called 'inner circle'. The more senior a Satanist becomes in his group, the more secrets are entrusted to him, and the greater the threat to the group if such a person escapes and/or reveals all. If such a member attempts to leave the group, physical threats and psychic attacks may be made upon him in order to keep him silent.

Sometimes an ex-Satanist may have to move home or change his whereabouts for two or three years after he has escaped from a Satanic temple. Many Satanists are single men, and a monastery or Christian community may be an appropriate milieu, so that help can always be guaranteed. Members of this community will need to be on their guard, especially until they are sure that the person who claims to be escaping is bona fide. Confidence tricksters and even Satanist infiltrators are far from unknown. A genuine and continuing Satanist will soon become uncomfortable within a Christian community, and will find it hard to keep up the regular round of Christian worship without evincing signs of distress.

The Satanist group will almost certainly try to get its old member back. Initially it will do so by playing on his sense of loyalty to the group through engineered encounters. If that does not succeed, there are techniques of intimidation, and even such drastic means as attempting to kidnap him with the help of sedative drugs or induced hypnosis. Anything will be tried, in order to keep him away from Christians. Certainly there will be some vindictive acts, certainly there will be attempts to discredit him and to sterilize anything he says; perhaps there may be dangerous practical jokes, threats to life or threats of injury, and psychological pressure.

Groups other than Satanist are less unscrupulous in their attempts to regain their old members, perhaps because they are basically well-intentioned and unlikely to bring themselves to the extremes to which Satanists are willing to go; perhaps because their 'secrets' are more accessible in printed publications on sale at occult bookshops; perhaps because occultists and magicians are basically less organized on anything other than a local level.

How can Christians help those who have been involved in occult or magical or Satanic practices, and who wish to renounce their former manner of life? The notes which follow will need to be modified according to the nature and degree of the person's involvement, and according to what particular system of belief he has been tied up with; but, in general:

1 They will have to be willing to break their allegiance with the group of which they were members, renounce the specific practices of which they have been guilty, renounce Satan and the vows they took in his temple (if they were Satanists), and turn to Jesus Christ as Lord.

2 This begins with a total confession of their past sin. For many, this will be their first use of confession with sacramental absolution at the

hands of a priest as God's representative. Along with the absolution there will need to be given a real assurance that God has completely forgiven and accepted them. It will be during the time of confession and challenge of commitment to Christ that the real battle with evil spiritual forces gripping the person's life will occur. Any evil forces restraining them from abandoning Satan for Christ will need to be:

(i) bound (Luke 11.17–26) in Jesus' name;
(ii) commanded to harm no one and to depart from the person (Luke 8.29; 4.36); and
(iii) commanded to go to the place that God has appointed for them (Matt. 8.29; Luke 8.31).

Following this turning to Christ, they will need to be baptized, or, if they are already baptized, to take their baptismal vows again, so reversing the rejection of Christ that their occult or Satanic practices involved. After baptism, the laying-on of hands and the anointing with oil (either at confirmation, or as part of the ministry of the local church to that person) should be performed, so that the person may remain full of the Holy Spirit, and be healed of all the evil work and bad memories of what has been wrought in his life previously. Liturgical forms for all this will be found in Appendix IV, especially in section VII on pages 128–32.

Real commitment to Christ will only be maintained by regular attendance at the Holy Communion, and involvement in Christian fellowship and community. Sustained follow-up is essential; a new Christian, if lonely and unsupported by friendly fellowship, can so easily become disillusioned and slip back into his old ways because he has not received the necessary encouragement from the Christian body. The counsellor who has helped that person back into the fold may not be able to do all this personally, because of his other commitments; but he should not be content until he has identified a small number of Christians who will make it their specific business to see that the convert receives the necessary help and friendship on a continuing basis.

Thereafter, the person who has been rescued from evil involvement should lead a regular God-centred prayer life with Bible reading and devotional exercises, and be willing to submit to Christian discipline. If we draw near to God the devil flees from us (Jas. 4.7–8), and we have access to God because of the work which Jesus accomplished on the cross (Eph. 1.7; Col. 1.20; Heb. 10.19). God puts his Holy Spirit round us as a protective wall of fire (Zech. 2.5), and his angels encamp around us (Ps. 91.11), to defend us from all evil.

8

Possession syndrome

Leaving aside for a moment the question of whether or not it is possible for a person to be possessed by an evil spirit, it is undoubtedly the case that he may *believe* that this is the case, and in many instances this belief is delusional in nature. In such a situation, the psychiatrist may talk of the 'possession syndrome', but will recognise it as a not uncommon concomitant of several different psychiatric disorders, and sometimes as the result of a disturbed group or family projecting their negative or wicked attributes on to an individual, whom they make their scapegoat and whom they persuade to believe himself possessed by the evil which in fact stems from the group itself.

Psychological projection is an important concept for the counsellor in this area to understand, as it is the key to many misperceptions of what is happening to the client. It is the name given to the process by which impulses, wishes, attitudes and other aspects of the self are unconsciously denied as belonging to the self and are attributed to someone (or something) else. There is a misinterpretation of inner mental activity and images, and a belief that they originate outside one's self and are external and objective events rather than internal and subjective states.

As with the projection of a film, the term 'projection' literally means a 'throwing in front of one's self'. The classic biblical illustration is the throwing of stones at the woman caught in the act of adultery (John 8.1–11); but no one is without sin, because 'whoever lusts after another also commits adultery in the heart' (Matt. 5.28), and therefore no one can cast the first stone. When we are thus exposed, it is clear that 'people in glass houses should not throw stones'!

The mental mechanism of splitting internal experiences and images into good and bad, white and black, and attributing them to the outside world, is a normal primitive function of the infant ego before the capacity to contain projections and integrate opposite states of mind has developed. It is also a natural defence of the ego against threatening affect, anxiety, conflict and guilt, and persists throughout life as an unconscious process. In analogy with the immune system of the body, it is activated to varying degrees according to the personality makeup of an individual or family, or because of group pressures, particular situations and stresses, and, most frankly, in mental disorder. It is not only bad, negative, unwanted aspects of the self which can be projected on to other individuals, groups or factions of society, but also good and valued qualities may be similarly projected. The idealization of the parent by the infant or small child is an example of this, as is the state of falling in love. When the self is faced with intolerable ambivalence or conflict, the opposites are split off, denied and projected according to the needs at the time of the ego of the individual, family or group. Thus stability is maintained.

It is through this process of projection (and often associated identification) that people actually may become controlled by others, and by the perceptions and beliefs of others. When this happens, it is not fanciful to use the term 'possession'. These mechanisms may also be represented in various forms of human bondage. In many of these cases, the responsible forces may be termed 'occult', at least in the sense that they are hidden from conscious awareness. The married daughter under her mother's thumb, the weak husband colluding with his domineering mother-in-law, the scapegoat at the office, the black sheep of the family, the 'unbeliever' in the house prayer group, may all be victims enmeshed by their assailants through the destructive forces of the mind. A case of projection involving cult membership will illustrate what is involved:

Case 25

A family asked for help in rescuing their eldest daughter from a 'love and peace' cult with whom she had become deeply involved. Her parents claimed that she had been brainwashed and had undergone a total personality change. The sad story emerged of how these decent and devoted parents had experienced enormous difficulties with their daughter during her adolescence. She had become delinquent and promiscuous, had left home, and had become caught up in a drugs and hippie scene. She had always been the less favoured child compared with her sister, and had taken on the role of rebel. There was not only a split in the family between the 'good' and 'bad' daughters, but also the 'bad' daughter had become split off from the rest of the family – as split off from them as their own darker natures were split off from themselves. She had become the carrier, into whom the others had projected their own undesirable qualities, particularly sexual and aggressive feelings, and she had been 'cast out' in order that the semblance of a happy home could be maintained. After a few years of unsavoury living, the daughter started looking for alternatives to satisfy the 'other side' of herself, since she needed to be loved and valued and to belong to a caring family. In this vulnerable state of 'near-conversion', she had fallen easy prey to a quasi-religious sect. Once she had been gathered up by this group and had taken on a state of dependence and subservience, she projected her own good qualities and her needs to be loved and valued into the charismatic sect leader, and all the negative attitudes and feelings onto the outside world. Like the other sect members, she had become an empty 'non-person' feeding the massive ego of the group and its leader, which saw itself united as a 'loving community' against a 'hostile uncaring society'.

As a general rule, therefore, no Christian should attempt to cast out a demon from a person unless he has good reason to believe that he is not confronted by a case of projection and possession syndrome. It is essential to take a detailed case history and make a thorough assessment of the physical, social, psychological and spiritual context within which the disturbance has arisen. This means that the Christian will work within a professional team handling the case. Many medically-based problems will be best dealt with by the person's general practitioner, but sometimes it will be necessary to collaborate with psychiatrist and social worker before a full diagnostic understanding can be gained and before a comprehensive plan of management can be devised – see especially the advice on pp. 118–19 below.

False possession may be recognized in a number of situations, of which the main ones are as follows:

1 *Occurring in the course of a major mental illness*

(a) *Schizophrenia* is the commonest basis in psychiatric experience for the belief that one is possessed, or being interfered with, by evil spirits. The illness is characterized by delusional thinking, hallucinations and experiences of being controlled and acted on by alien forces which may be interpreted as demons who are attacking or possessing the sufferer. The symptoms may take on a floridly religious colouring, being misinterpreted as the work of a punishing God or as attacks by the devil. There may be visions, voices, tactile hallucinations, or vile smells, but they all originate within the sufferer, who is experiencing his own internal

73

thoughts and feelings as if they were outside himself and the work of external entities. The associated delusional interpretation and conse-quent behaviour invariably have a bizarre quality. This condition is quite different from ecstatic or religious experience. It is persistent, and tends to pervade the person's life and relationships in an indiscriminate fashion. It is an experience which is not integrating, life-giving, or life-enhancing, but rather, monotonous, unfulfilling, like a record stuck in a groove.

(b)   A person suffering from *depressive psychosis* (or, less often, from manic and mixed affective illness) may complain of being possessed or attacked by the devil or demons. The extreme changes experienced in these affective illnesses may be accompanied by abnormal behaviour, delusions, disturbances in perception and even hallucinations that have been misinterpreted as the work of evil beings. A severely depressed mood often carries with it an overwhelming sense of blackness, guilt and unworthiness. There is alway the risk of suicide (particularly when there are ideas of guilt and nihilism, and hypochondriacal features). When other people are incorporated into the person's delusional thinking, homicide is also a very real danger. Depressive illness and paranoid psychoses (and schizophrenia, but to a lesser extent) may also affect a couple who are living together, so that they begin to construct and develop a highly collusive state of unreality (*folie à deux*) which may be unwittingly fed by the attitudes and responses of others. In these circumstances, the belief in evil oppression or possession may become extremely persuasive, and 'take in' outside counsellors as well (*folie à trois*, etc.).

(c)   Frightening experiences of evil and of demons may occur in the course of an *organic psychosis*. Organic conditions may produce mental symptoms of 'possession by evil forces or demons' which are largely shaped by the person's pre-morbid personality and belief system. Psychotic states may arise during the course of medical conditions (for example, thyroid disease) and treatments (for example, post–operative states, steroid therapy), or in association with alcoholism and drug intoxications. Some forms of epilepsy, migraine aura and brain tumours may produce features which could be wrongly taken for possession.

2   *Neurotic and personality disorders*

(a)   Neurotic disorders and serious maladjustments of personality may show characteristics attributed to possession. In *hysterical neurosis*, the processes of dissociation and conversion reactions result from inner psychological conflict, with the purpose of relieving intense and unbearable anxiety. In the case of hysterical conversion reaction, though the person may complain of being possessed, the symbolic meaning of the reaction may often be elicited. In the dissociative states, and in the rare cases of split or multiple personality syndrome, the dramatic manifestations of unconscious mental activity may make a demonic interpretation much more plausible. As a result of the decomposition of the principal ego function, sub-personalities such as are normally contained in the unconscious minds of all individuals may emerge as characters of their own, seemingly quite separate from the principal ego, and interpreted as invading entities. If they are particularly ugly, shadowy or inhuman in nature, they may well be misinterpreted as evil spirits who have taken possession of the victim.

(b)   Apart from neurotic disturbances, some individuals may have a more pervasive *hysterical personality disorder* characterized by a craving for attention, sensation and dramatization. Fantastic stories concerning the occult are guaranteed to stimulate curiosity, so they are invented in order to attract attention. The person may become so convinced of his tales that he even deceives himself into believing them. He is not so likely to mislead others to whom he tells them, although in the most malignant form of this disorder of personality, there may be confidence tricksters who can involve many people in their schemes.

(c)   Many apparently healthy individuals may have aspects of their personality, or life experiences, which the conscious mind considers to be undesirable. They are contained in the unconscious mind as *repressed material*. Such material may rear up under conditions of stress at some stage and, because it is unacceptable to the conscious mind, it is recognized by the sufferer and observer, not in its true form as subconscious material, but in the guise of extraneous influences. Base or unwanted aspects of personality, acted out seemingly against the will of the sufferer, or beyond his conscious control, may be thus expressed. They can be so ugly and out of character that they are interpreted as demons within the person, or as apparitions and other manifestations in his environment. This may come about during a highly exciting and emotionally-charged group experience, when normal ego control and the normal defence mechanism of repression is loosened. Shamanistic initiation ceremonies may be an example of this; so may certain of the more excitable manifestations of charismatic religious activity.

3 *The poltergeist*

As has already been said (pages 17–18 above), poltergeist phenomena which disturb certain families are another form of dissociated mental activity or energy, not the activity of a geist who is poltering about. This often bizarre form of the acting-out of interpersonal tensions is always unconscious (except when manufactured for fraudulent motives) and of human origin. It may be offered as material for exorcism when psychological management is really indicated.

All these cases require specialized assessment and management, and no form of exorcism should be attempted. It will be potentially extremely harmful. Medical or psychological treatment is primary, but spiritual counselling and sacramental healing, where appropriate, are a timely contribution to the whole care of the person.

There are other occasions when possession may be claimed, but the true diagnosis may well be possession syndrome rather than possession itself. Three deserve particular mention:

Bereavement reactions. Counsellors will be familiar with bereavement reactions and the usual process of mourning, but grief may sometimes be complicated by serious disturbances in perception and a condition resembling mental illness. The whole picture may be compounded by the effects of involvement with spiritualism. If the bereaved person has a bad conscience about this involvement, he may well interpret the bereavement reaction as the effect upon him of invading malign spirit entities, and ask that he be exorcized of them. Bereavement counselling must be the foundation of any approach to treatment of such cases, whether the main thrust of the treatment be psychiatric management of a reactive illness, depth psychotherapy to release suppressed anger and guilt, sacramental healing, deliverance or a requiem Eucharist. All forms of therapy fall short without full spiritual completion, and none more so than in the afflictions of bereavement.

Occult involvement. Varying degrees of mental disturbance can result from involvement in occult practices such as ouija, tarot, divining, spiritualism, etc. In some cases, there may be a predisposition to mental imbalance which leads the person into these activities and is in turn accentuated by them. The leading symptoms and their severity will determine the approach to treatment. No opportunity should be lost of delivering the afflicted person from darkness to light, but exorcism as such will rarely, if ever, be the right form of treatment.

Charismatic casualties. The decline in supportive social networks has seen the growth of many different charismatic groups and sects, some with a highly developed demonology and exorcistic practice. Although there is a high prevalence of psychological and spiritual distress among those joining such sects, there is much to show that serious disturbances can result from the impact of groups on individuals. In particular, the more zealous groups may become enmeshed in psychological and spiritual manipulation, with the most tragic consequences.

The majority of psychiatrists will probably regard all experiences attributed to possession as symptoms of various forms of mental imbalance or disturbance. A minority may be prepared to admit either that possession is a possible explanation in rare cases, or at least that they can offer no explanation for some aspects of experiences attributed to possession. Even in those cases where priest and psychiatrist can both entertain the possibility of possession as a true explanation, it is usually found that psychological conflicts, relationship problems and psychiatric symptoms are also present and may often be prominent. Such people will benefit from conventional psychiatric treatment or management, whatever else on a spiritual level may be done to cope with possession. Any case diagnosed as needing exorcism, therefore, is likely to have its psychiatric aspect, and co-operation between priest and medical practitioner is essential if the whole patient is to be cured. Further advice about the relationship between priest and psychiatrist is given in Appendix III, especially on pages 118–19.

Case 26

A fifty-year-old woman was admitted to a psychiatric hospital claiming to be possessed. She said that the devil had taken her over and was directing her thoughts and actions. She spent most of her time crying and claiming that she could see the devil in the form of a ram's head. She was diagnosed as a monosymptomatic psychotic, but failed to improve after various drug therapies. Her psychiatrist, because the patient was in such deep distress and because of the nature of her symptoms, decided to call in a priest. The patient became very frightened at the priest's presence, as she believed she was not worthy to be with so holy a person. She was totally obsessed with her own unworthiness and sin. She was, after due counselling, prepared for confession and exorcism. The psychiatrist felt that these feelings of possession might be linked with the fact that she had been married late in life to a man who had been her lover for many years, and that she had a very deep-seated guilt problem. The rite of exorcism was carried out at the request of the psychiatrist, but the patient continued to show signs of psychotic illness. Her symptoms were to some extent alleviated with the help of drugs, but she still believed that she was possessed and damned.

Case 27

A young graduate obtained his first job in London, but felt very lonely there. He met a group of charismatic Christians and was impressed by their love and concern, so he sought to join them. He realized he was required to 'speak in tongues' and show other outward signs of charismatic renewal. In time the group appeared to realize that he was a rather weak and lonely person with many personal problems, and they began to make him a scapegoat for problems which arose within the group. Eventually they decided that he was 'possessed', and they carried out a rite of exorcism in which he was physically assaulted and frightened. He remembers rolling on the ground, quite convinced that the devil was in him and that they were trying to drive it out. Following that experience, he went to see his local vicar who was able to integrate him into the local church and congregation, and also to help him cope with the harassment which he received as a result of leaving the house church.

Case 28

(This and the following case are reprinted from 'Psychiatry and the occult' by J. Guy Edwards and David Gill, in *The Practitioner*, vol. 225 (January 1981), page 86, by permission of the Editor.)

A twenty-nine-year-old man with a personality disorder had a psychotic episode in which he heard drumming and groaning, and believed that witchcraft ceremonies were being held in an adjacent room in a Spanish holiday resort. The episode followed a period of heavy drinking of cheap wine, in which the patient ate very little food. In the past he had read practically all of Dennis Wheatley's novels, which presumably influenced the content of his psychotic experiences. Interest in the occult can colour the content of perceptual experiences of epileptic origin in a similar way.

Case 29

(See the note prefacing the previous case.)

Organic and psychogenic symptomatology can, of course, exist side by side. This is exemplified by the case of a seventeen-year-old girl who had had true epilepsy, hysterical epileptiform fits and consciously feigned attacks. Her bizarre behaviour at school was alien to her gentle disposition. Because her 'epileptic attacks' were not successfully treated, the rumour that she was possessed by a demon spread within the school. Children and teachers described how they had a strange feeling in her presence, as if someone inside was looking through her eyes and laughing at them. Psychiatric explorations revealed that her strict parents never allowed her to ventilate her feelings through normal channels and that a grief reaction after the death of her grandmother was unresolved. Her abnormal behaviour disappeared after treatment along psychotherapeutic lines. The case also illustrates how, even in this day and age, atypical manifestations of an illness may be explained in a primitive way.

Case 30

The relatives of a thirty-year-old woman described how, four years previously, spirits were successfully invoked in sessions on the ouija board. The woman became acutely frightened and distressed and was no longer able to stay alone, always seeking the company of others at night. Her husband was away in the Navy. She claimed that she was hearing footsteps, seeing faces and was unable to sleep. The general practitioner who saw her at the time felt that she was in a 'hysterical' state, and found that the agitation responded to Valium. She said that she enjoyed communicating with the spirits but that she became frightened when she heard footsteps up the stairs and experienced a strange smell like that of a corpse in the house. The footsteps were also heard by her sister. The furniture seemed to have been interfered with, and she had seen a man standing by her bed in the early hours of the morning. The man who contacted her through the ouija board was a gentleman whom she had nursed prior to his death. Subsequently she became very disturbed, and was unable to look after her children or stay alone in the house. When seen by psychiatrists she was in an agitated mental state in which she was preoccupied with various spiritualistic ideas and with the conviction that her house was haunted. A month later she was acutely distressed and depressed, and was admitted to hospital uttering statements such as 'I am going to die in two hours' time', 'I am condemned as a traitor', 'I have blasphemed', 'I am guilty'. She showed markedly regressive behaviour and she was obsessed by voices whispering in her ears and tormenting her. She would walk round the ward distraught, tearful, and having plugged her ears with paper to keep out the voices. Initially, treatment with electro-convulsive therapy seemed to lift the depression, but she still continued to hear voices and claimed to be under attack from them. Later she was treated in another hospital where the psychiatrists were convinced of the diagnosis of schizophrenia, and accordingly treated her with phenothiazines. The parish priest and diocesan adviser believed possession to be a possibility. An exorcism was performed. After this, and with continued psychiatric treatment, she made a good recovery. The caring work of the Christian community supporting her was most impressive.

Case 31

Help was sought by the relatives of a fifty-two-year-old woman because they believed her to be under the influence of evil spirits. Her son described her as a kind, attentive mother who gradually lost the self-confidence to step out from her home situation and to lead a more varied and open life. Once her son had left home, she became discontented with her home environment and seemed unable to find a solution to her dilemma. At a family party, a ouija board seance was held for fun, but afterwards she began to pursue this activity on her own, and it seemed to take over her life. She received messages through the ouija board and later heard voices indicating that a

'Prince Charming' in the spirit world was interested in her and would soon take her away on a romantic journey. On one occasion, she packed her suitcase and went to the lay-by of a nearby motorway, believing that her 'Prince Charming' would meet her and she would then be married to him. When seen by a psychiatrist, she seemed completely caught up by these fanciful beliefs. She had ceased doing her housework and she and her husband were living completely separate lives. In fact, she denied that he was her husband, referring to him as 'that man'. At first she was inaccessible to therapy, saying, 'Don't you try to psychiatric me'. Later she revealed a deep sadness, that she believed she had married the wrong man, that she had not been able to adjust to her only son's growing up and leaving home, and had been unable to make for herself a satisfying and purposeful life once he had gone. The diagnosis which was proffered was that she was suffering from hysterical pseudo-psychosis which provided an escape from the hardships of reality and prevented her from satisfactorily resolving her underlying conflicts. No exorcism was either suggested or attempted.

9

Possession

When all the foregoing cases of possession syndrome or pseudo-possession have been described, there is still a residue of cases where the only remaining diagnosis is the activity of an evil spirit, and for which the only effective remedy will be that of exorcism, frequently carried out concomitantly with psychiatric treatment. There is a spectrum of demonic activity:

1   Every Christian knows that he is subject to *temptation*.

2   Temptation may become so intense that it has to be described as demonic *obsession*. In this state, temptation and demonic interference increases to such a degree that normal life begins to become impossible because of ideas in the mind, a preoccupation with evil, or a sense of all-pervading guilt or fear.

3   A further stage may be called *oppression*, in which there is occult or demonic attack in dreams or otherwise.

4   *Possession* is the most serious case. In this, the person's will is taken over by an intruding alien entity. When this happens, the person is incapable of asking for deliverance on his own behalf. It may be a temporary state, however, so that the person when he is not possessed may know that he has been, and so will come to a counsellor expressing a wish to be released from this recurring condition. If a person is possessed by a demon, it can only be dislodged by exorcism.

Possession is not so common as the media like to make out. It cannot just 'happen' unwittingly. Man cannot catch demons as he catches the common cold. He has to put himself at risk and in a vulnerable position. The greatest risk is that of straightforward invitation. This can occur knowingly, by membership of a voodoo, witchcraft, magic or Satanist group, by 'do it yourself' magic experiments, or by the deliberate invitation extended from a despairing will. It can come about unknowingly by fringe occultism of various descriptions such as the ouija board, planchette or other 'sessions' or seances in which the operator opens himself to possible invasion by some external spirit. There may also (but rarely) be cases where the invitation is very indirect, where the victim may be an empty soul with no particular faith to withstand stray spiritual influences of a malign kind, and has put himself in a position of danger without realizing the danger in which he stands. Possession may sometimes come about through some kind of occult transference from a Satanist group or witch coven, or by cursing, or possibly genetically through long family occult traditions.

The diagnosis of possession

(The remainder of this chapter, as far as the illustrative cases, is reproduced, with permission, from pages 44–9 of *A Handbook for Christian Exorcists* by Douglas Howell-Everson, privately published in 1982 and now out of print. A few minor alterations have been made in the course of discussion with the Christian Exorcism Study Group.)

If the exorcist can discover, or *un*cover them, one or several of the following causes will be found to lie in the background history of the patient.

1 *The background causes*

(a) A blatant and unrepentant life of selfish sin.

(b) Occultism of some form, where an invitation is wittingly given to occult powers, or some sacrifice or incantation is made.

(c) Deliberate subjection to a Satanic or Luciferian cult, or worship of a 'life-force'.

(d) An outlook of totally self-centred materialism.

(e) Occultism in the family, causing the patient to be dedicated to – or baptized into – some demonic cult, in infancy.

(f) A desire for some person, thing or power, combined with a willingness to pay the price, i.e. the surrender of the will to demonic powers in return for a 'reward'. It should be understood that the person who offers to pay the price may not realize that payment will eventually have to be exacted, or may think that he can escape without paying.

2 *The signs of demonic oppression*

(a)   There will be a rapid change in the characteristics of the thoughts and feelings of the patient:

   (i)   An indifference, amounting to repulsion, to spiritual influence for good, and a rejection of any possibility of belief in a good God;

   (ii)   the mind becomes filled with a continuous stream of evil thoughts and anti-Christian ideas and desires;

   (iii)   the patient is consumed with a passion for senseless and pointless lying, so strong that it becomes automatic;

   (iv)   although he feels no remorse for the background causes, the patient is plagued with a continual restlessness, lack of inner peace, and depressive moods;

   (v)   he finds Christian symbolism disturbing and upsetting;

   (vi)   terrible paranoid fears are frequent, and a common symptom is that there is someone or something with him, though not *in* him, day and night.

(b)   His conscious will becomes secondary to the control of some more powerful will. He is aware of this but cannot explain it satisfactorily:

   (i)   He feels compelled to do what he knows and recognizes as wrong, no matter how much he dislikes it;

   (ii)   he will manifest sudden and unaccountable fits of fury and blasphemy, coupled with a defiant and aggressive attitude to other people;

   (iii)   his contacts with other people will be punctuated by outbreaks of causeless spite, enmity, excitability and violent behaviour. When angered, he curses aloud – both the object of his rage and himself – and compromise and reconciliation is unknown to, and impossible with, him;

   (iv)   for no apparent reason, in cold blood, he may find himself striking, or even attempting to kill, his friends and relatives;

   (v)   there will be a consuming desire for narcotics, alcohol, nicotine, and for abnormal sexual relationships, and this desire or craving will be different in kind from anything that the patient has experienced before, while he will be aware that there will be no satisfaction to be gained by the gratification of the craving;

(vi)   he will have an urge to hurt or destroy his own body, and there will be no masochistic pleasure in any hurt he does;

(vii)   under stress he may actually call out the name of Satan in the same way that a normal unthinking man, under stress, may call out 'Oh God', or 'Christ';

(viii)   this will be coupled with the fact that he will be unable to speak or write the name of Jesus without a fierce effort. If forced to say it, he will only be able to do so after a great effort, and with a disgusted or distorted expression and in a mechanical voice. Indeed, after hearing or while hearing it, he may glower or become excited or aggressive;

(ix)   if invited to pray, he may be unable to force himself to make the ritual actions associated with prayer – kneeling, folding the hands, closing the eyes – while a feeling of choking, or a series of overwhelmingly blasphemous thoughts fill his consciousness;

(x)   he will avoid all talk of demons and switch the conversation should such a subject be mentioned;

(xi)   all forms of spiritual assistance make him restless and unfriendly;

(xii)   he may suddenly develop supernormal extra-sensory or other powers.

(c)   He will be conscious of bitter inner conflict when given spiritual advice or when in contact with spiritual objects:

(i)   Although he will be conscious of his sins, he will be unable to be sorry about them, nor will he be able to make any reparation or sign of repentance, nor resist seriously the temptation to repeat them;

(ii)   he will be unable to recognize God as a loving and forgiving figure;

(iii)   he will feel uncomfortable in the presence of Christian friends or helpers, and his behaviour to them will alternate daily between insolence and spite on the one hand and extreme dependence on the other. Some of them he may drop suddenly for no apparent reason except that they have become repugnant to him;

85

(iv) if he attends a church service, it may be impossible for him to prevent himself laughing aloud, jeering or even being sick, and murderous thoughts will fill his mind;

(v) if he attempts to pray or to read some devotional matter, revulsion will overcome him or he may suddenly feel complete exhaustion and prostration. In any event, his concentration will vanish and will be replaced by clear and vivid distractions. The observer will note that he is unable to remain in a devotional posture and may suddenly spring up, explaining with some anger that it is all meaningless and time-wasting;

(vi) his inner conflict will often be a source of great pain and unease to him, as he will not understand the reason why vile suggestions seem to come into his mind. If he does appreciate that their origin is diabolic, he will feel restless either because he is resisting, or because he feels guilty in *not* resisting.

3 *The signs of demonic possession*

The patient will show all the above signs of demonic obsession very much magnified and, in addition, the following signs will be observed:

(a) There will be physical signs, such as a bilious complexion, wasting of the body and psychosomatic pains, all unassociated with any particular illness, and an evil or frightening expression will become habitual.

(b) Conversation on Christian subjects or the presence of Christian religious symbols will be unbearable to the patient and will cause sudden screaming, cursing, raving, grinding of teeth and generally violent behaviour. He will laugh or jeer even at overheard conversations on Christian subjects.

(c) When blessed, or prayed for, he may fall into a type of trance-state in which he will manifest one of the three characteristic signs:

(i)   He speaks in a voice unlike his normal voice;
(ii) in a language, or languages, unknown to him in his normal state;
(iii) he will be able to converse in that language and answer questions if they are put to him.

He will be completely unaware of what has happened when he recovers from that state.

(d)   At times, *and especially when confronted by the exorcist*, he will display preternatural strength, quite beyond what could be expected from his physical condition, manifesting itself in gusts of violent rage.

(e)   He will show extraordinary powers of clairvoyance, being able to recount accurately things and events happening at a distance in time or space (for example, details of the past history or childhood of the exorcist) which he could not otherwise know.

(f)   There may well be other psychic phenomena – for example, poltergeist manifestations in his vicinity, especially at night.

(g)   When exorcism is about to take place, he may see and/or hear demonic and terrible figures speaking, and threatening him.

4   *The patient's reaction to the exorcist*

This will be similar in both conditions, obviously magnified in the second. The object of the demon will be to prevent any exorcism from taking place, and this he will do either by trying to conceal his presence for as long as possible, or, later, by endeavouring to sow discord and distrust between the exorcist and the patient, and discouragement in the heart of the exorcist.

The patient may be willing to discuss his case, although he will avoid any mention of the demonic and may even start to confess his connection with the occult, but will then suddenly exhibit marked distrust and refuse to continue. As an alternative, he may find that his mind goes completely blank, or that he is rendered speechless for a considerable length of time, or he will suddenly remember some reason for terminating his contact with the exorcist.

If the conversation reaches the point of his own sins and misdeeds, he may cover his face with his hands, for it will become distorted with anger, or he will simply refuse to speak, or deny what he has previously admitted, or accuse the exorcist of speaking of these things only in order to shame and despise the patient.

His attitude will be summed up by the following remarks: 'Admit that this is all a waste of time and that I am only a burden to you; all you are doing is trying to blackmail me into talking to you, and I shall only tell you lies anyway.'

A female patient may suddenly become extremely seductive and endeavour to confuse the exorcist by sexual provocation or, alternatively, accuse the exorcist of sexual attempts on her. The patient will be completely unable to pray any meaningful prayer for help, or of penitence, and his condition will progressively worsen as he uncovers his inner conflict.

Immediately before exorcism, there will probably be violence and a complete disorganization of bodily control, leading to vomiting, urination, defecation and apparent syncope.

Case 32

A twenty-four-year-old girl was admitted to a psychiatric clinic, claiming that she was possessed. She was showing some of the traditional signs of possession, for example the ability to speak in a foreign language of which she had no previous knowledge, and an unusual knowledge of events. The psychiatrists were divided as to whether she was suffering from a neurotic or psychotic condition, but agreed that a priest should be involved in the case. The priest saw the patient interviewed by two psychiatrists and then interviewed the patient herself. When the priest entered the room, the patient (without knowing of his visit) knew his name and where he was from and that he was an exorcist. It was agreed that the rite of exorcism should be carried out. During this, the patient convulsed and spoke in the voice of three different men, claiming to be Lust, Greed and Death. These spirits were exorcized one at a time, after which the girl collapsed and lost consciousness for a short while. On gaining consciousness, she asked for something to eat, and appeared to be quite normal.

Case 33

Susan was recruited into a group which some people believe to be of a Satanist nature, at the age of fifteen, while living in London. She later went to a university in the north of England, during which time she rose to a position of local leadership in this group. In her final year at university, she met a Christian who offered her help to leave the organization if she wanted to become a Christian. After long discussion this happened, and the Christian took Susan to see a priest. The priest prayed with Susan, who suddenly went into a trance, hissed, and curled off the chair across the room like a snake. The priest pronounced an exorcism, and within some seconds Susan felt free. For some time she continued to have problems with the members of her former group, who tried to get her back, but some Christians who offered help arranged to protect her until she felt strong enough in herself, and the group's interest in her had waned.

Case 34

The exorcist was called in by the relatives of the possessed woman, who had been for many years a member of a witch coven centred on the country village in which she had lived all her life. The possessed was a middle-aged woman of limited intelligence and working-class status. She had never left the isolated village in her life except for shopping in the neighbouring market town. *Immediately* the exorcist entered the room, she started calling out details of his past life which he thought he had forgotten and which were relevant to a wild youth. The second priest in the team had served for many years in the Middle East and was an Arabic scholar. He questioned the woman in various Arabic dialects, and she replied in those dialects. Neither the past of the exorcist nor the dialects could have been known to this woman by any rational process. After exorcism she lost these extra-sensory powers and renounced her witchcraft.

10

Exorcism

Exorcism of places

It is probably easier to establish that a particular place needs treatment because of the activity of evil spirits than it is correctly to diagnose demonic possession in the case of a person. Having said that, it is certainly much more difficult to ascertain what treatment a disturbed place needs, since one type of haunt tends to overlap another. The exorcist should therefore always be prepared to find that his initial treatment of a place has not been of complete benefit and that it has disposed of certain phenomena and not of others. The results of his initial treatment will help to indicate the root cause of the disturbance.

There are three distinct 'weapons' in the hands of the exorcist: blessing, lesser exorcism and greater exorcism.

(i) To *bless* a place is to call down upon it the forces of God and of goodness. Blessing may be combined with an aspersion of the place with holy water. These acts can never do harm, will always do good, and invariably give comfort to those who have been distressed at what is happening in the disturbed place.

(ii) The *lesser exorcism* is a sequence of prayers to God, asking him to deliver that place from all evils which may be affecting it, and will fulfil the requirements of most cases presented to the exorcist when he feels that some form of liberation is required by the circumstances but he is not sure that a specific evil spirit has actually taken up its permanent abode in the place concerned.

(iii) The *greater exorcism* (sometimes called a 'major exorcism') is a direct command to demons or demonic forces in the name of Christ, requiring them to depart from that place for ever, to go to their own place, and not to harm any human beings (living or departed) as they do so. The greater exorcism only affects demons, so should only be used in those cases where the exorcist is convinced that demons are active and in charge. Such cases will be rare. The greater exorcism should only be used with the direct and express permission and knowledge of the diocesan bishop.

Even when he does not suspect the activity of explicit demonic forces, the exorcist should never leave a place to which he has been called without taking some remedial action to ease the minds of the people concerned. In the case of poltergeist phenomena in a household where none of the members is an active Christian, it may not be appropriate to pray with the members of the household. It is essential, however, to counsel them as to the likely aetiology of the disturbance, and to assure them that the exorcist himself will be praying for them over the next few days (and at least until his next visit, if he has promised to 'look in' again). If Christians are involved, there should always be prayer with them as well as for them. They have a right to expect it of a representative of Christ in his Church, when he calls to carry out the ministry of Christ which has been requested for a particular place. In the case of a simple place memory, there will be no need for any exorcism, but – once the nature of the place memory has been explained and the explanation has been grasped – the house and its inhabitants should be blessed. The act of blessing should noticeably calm down the atmosphere of fear and discord which caused the exorcist to be invited in the first place. In all cases it will be appropriate to offer Christian pastoral care and support, either by the priest or by a member or members of his congregation.

Whatever ritual act is decided upon to meet any particular case, it should be carefully explained to all those present (especially in the case of dwelling houses), so that everyone can be associated by prayer and sacramental act with the actual cleansing process. This is especially important, since few disturbances of this kind are individual; all affect the whole family, and it is the family unit to which the ministry of Christ is being offered. It is possible that, at this stage, personal problems which have not already been disclosed during interviews may become apparent. The exorcist and his team should be aware of these possibilities and be ready to intervene. Until all the work of counselling has been done, the way is not clear for acts of deliverance.

Where there have been attacks on a church building, resulting in the scrawling (or performance) of obscenities within consecrated premises, or attempts at desecration of the altar, or the appearance of symbols which are suspected of being occult or Satanic, it is necessary to perform some act which will counter the attempted desecration. Sometimes it is not easy to tell whether a church building has been subjected to mere mindless vandalism or to specific and evilly-directed attack on the spiritual level. If the attack seems to be directed towards the altar or the aumbry rather than towards the alms-box or the Mothers' Union banner, it is more likely to be Satanically inspired. Vandals and arsonists look for different targets than Satanists, though the mentally unstable may attack the altar and the sacrament as a part of their psychosis, and the results may be indistinguishable from a Satanic attempt at desecration.

In none of these cases, however, is it appropriate to think of reconsecration of the building, or to speak in such terms. Consecration, like baptism, avails for all time and cannot be repeated. What is required is an action which cleanses the building of all attempted defilement and restores it to its pristine spiritual condition. (This is sometimes spoken of as the 'reconciliation' of the building.) A Eucharist with the lesser exorcism, and aspersion of the four walls of the building, should suffice.

The amount of publicity should be commensurate with the publicity accorded the original defilement. To make a great public fuss about what is known only to a small number of people would be to accord the forces of evil an importance which they may desire but do not deserve. If (as often happens) the disturbance to the building is known only to a few people, then the cleansing and blessing should be carried out by the parish priest and a small number of trusted friends and parishioners. If the whole congregation has been publicly aware of what has been done to the church, then the whole congregation should be involved in the remedial action.

A major exorcism will be appropriate only in the rare case of demonic infestation of a building. The infestation will have been brought about by human agency, often by the habitual use of the place for occult practices, pagan worship, witch covens, or animal sacrifice. It must be approached and treated with great caution. An exorcist should never work on his own. He needs the support and protection of a team of reputable and experienced helpers. His bishop should know what he is about, and the prayer support of a group of Christians or a religious community is invaluable.

The characteristic of a place needing a greater exorcism is the overwhelming atmosphere of evil and terror which cannot fail to affect all in its vicinity. Christian symbols will be attacked and desecration attempted. The victims of the interference find that they are unable, without the utmost difficulty, to make any specific Christian act such as praying, reading the Bible, or meditation. Those under attack will observe unaccountable and hostile happenings and a rapid deterioration in their relationships with other people. This will be displayed in outbursts of rage or panic – terror at the worst and manifestations of spite and envy at the least. Persons who are ripe for demonic domination, or subject to it, are naturally greatly at risk, but there will be, for all about the place, feelings akin to those of the threat of death and destruction. The place may well acquire a record of unaccountable actions and even of suicide. It is understandable that in such an atmosphere of strain, severe mental disturbance will not be uncommon.

The exorcist will either be subjected to the full blast of demonic fury, in which case he will be at major physical risk himself, or, alternatively, he will find that his arrival produces a spurious peace which will last until some definite move is made to exorcize the place. This will happen when the demon responsible has attempted to pretend that the situation does not require qualified attention. Because of the concomitant psychological disturbance which is being caused to persons and families in the vicinity, there will often also be poltergeist phenomena in the place. Their characteristic aimlessness will, however, in this case, be less in evidence; there will be a tendency for the phenomena to be directed against specifically Christian objects.

The team must be prepared to meet strong opposition of both a spiritual and a psychic nature. Team members may also experience physical violence. If they are attempting to exorcize a place which has been used for Satanic rites, and there are threats of physical violence made anonymously (by letter or by telephone call) the police should be informed. Once the matter has been explained to them, they will be more than willing to co-operate.

So far as spiritual and psychic violence is concerned, the team must make careful and adequate preparation beforehand. This should include confession, absolution and the celebration of a Eucharist with special intention for the work ahead. Never underestimate the strength of the forces you expect to meet when engaged in this kind of operation. Any member of the team who feels unable to take part in the operation should be excused without questioning or hesitation, and should be reassured that there will be no attachment of blame or shame on him for so doing.

The question is sometimes asked whether a person (priest or lay person) can properly take part in a ceremony of exorcism if he himself does not believe in the personalization of evil in the form of demons, or if he does not believe that the particular case with which he is involved is the result of the activity of demonic entities. The answer is that Christ knows the demons, and he knows whether in a particular case demons are involved. It is Christ who casts the demons out; they know him and his power; the exorcist acts not on his own authority or by reason of his own understanding but as the human agent of Christ. The agnostic can therefore act 'as if ', offering up his own work and carrying out the work of Christ. Providing he puts himself completely at the disposal of Christ in this ministry, he can rely upon Christ to make up any deficiencies in his ministry and to over-rule any misinterpretations on the part of his human agent.

The operation of the major exorcism of a place should be carried out in the following manner:

1   Make reconnaissance of the place, see that all animals and children are removed from the premises, and, if it is indoors, wedge all doors and cupboards firmly open.

2   Exorcize immediately, using an imperative form of words (see the formulae suggested in section IV of Appendix IV on page 125) in as many places as the exorcist feels necessary. There should be a second priest ready to take over at once if the first is prevented in any way. It is advisable to have the words of the formula written out and in the exorcist's hand, to prevent the evil spirit from so confusing the exorcist that he finds it impossible to remember the words he is intent on using. The exorcism must continue whatever happens or appears to happen, and whomever or whatever is threatened, until all opposition of any kind has ceased.

3   Meanwhile, the remainder of the team must maintain continuous mental prayer throughout the operation. They need at all times to bear in mind that they are fighting an actual battle against the powers of evil, but that they are protected by a far superior power because they are the vanguard of the irresistible army of Christ.

4   Once the exorcism has been completed, the place should be blessed and aspersed, room by room. The object of the exercise is not only to remove the powers of evil, but to fill the place with the presence of Christ. A room left empty after one devil has been cast out is an invitation for seven worse ones to come and take over (Matt. 12.43–5).

5   Those concerned must next make an immediate and total renunciation of all Satanic or occult worship, explicit or implicit, and must, in the presence of the team, remove and burn any manuscript, books or objects connected with such worship. The exorcist should asperge and

remove anything which cannot be burnt, and dispose of it completely and without delay.

6   Anyone who, in the course of Satanic or witchcraft rituals, has renounced Christian baptism, must in turn renounce his Satanic or witchcraft name and be formally received back into the Christian Church.

7   Aftercare is essential. All persons concerned should be instructed in the practice of God-centred prayer; simple prayers should be written out for them to use every day. The parish priest should do all in his power to integrate the victims firmly within a supportive Christian congregation, where they can grow spiritually within the ambience of Christian practice. It is usually advisable to ensure that a small number of members of the congregation is given the specific task of befriending the person or family concerned, and helping to provide Christian nurture.

8   A complete and detailed report should be submitted to the diocesan bishop under whose ultimate authority the whole exorcism will have been carried out.

Case 35

A particular parish had a long tradition, both within the church community and the village, of being 'difficult' and characterized by unhappy relationships. The priest who was helping out in the parish during a vacancy between incumbents heard tell of psychic disturbances in the ancient church – a sense of oppression, the feeling of a presence near the font at the back of the church, the crashing-to of the main door while the organist was practising in the empty church or people were going about their business in the vestry. Research revealed that ancient maps of the area showed numerous sites in the vicinity which could have been used for pagan and cult worship. In all probability, the church itself had been built on an ancient pagan site at the highest point in the neighbourhood. There were two Saxon 'crosses' in the church; one of these had pagan carvings and no suggestion of Christian symbolism. A Eucharist was arranged at which the building was exorcized. All went smoothly until the 'pagan' cross was approached. Here, tremendous resistance was sensed, and it was only with great difficulty (experienced by all present) that the rite was completed. The following Sunday,

95

members of the congregation expressed surprise at the way in which the whole church seemed lighter, warmer, different, cleaner than hitherto. No one knew of the exorcism except the priest concerned, the diocesan adviser, and those whom he had invited to the exorcism. When the new incumbent was inducted the archdeacon looked knowingly at the priest concerned and said: 'I think you have removed something from this church recently without the authority of a faculty.' Pastoral relationships and Christian work in the parish under the new incumbent have since improved considerably. It is interesting to note that the 'difficulty' in both village and church dated from the 1870s, at which time the two Saxon stones had been brought inside the church from their original positions, the better to protect them against weather and vandalism.

Exorcism of persons

As with places, so with people. There are many possible treatments for those who are troubled by psychic and occult disturbances, or who have been involved in traffic with demonic powers. Prayer and blessing, the laying-on of hands and/or anointing may be sufficient, and are always appropriate. Exorcism may be positively harmful if it is not the right treatment. It should be reserved for those cases where non-human malevolent influence is suspected. Human spirits, whether incarnate, earthbound or departed, should not be exorcized. They need, not banishment to hell, but love and concern and pastoral concern. When a person is disturbed by the attentions of discarnate humans, prayer, blessing and the requiem Eucharist are more appropriate than attempts at banishment.

We have seen in the foregoing pages that there should always be collaboration with medical opinion before the diagnosis of demonic influence is accepted. When exorcism seems to be proper (and such cases will be rare) there can be a *minor* or a *major* exorcism. Minor exorcisms are common and can be frequent. The Lord's Prayer itself, with its petition to 'deliver us from [the] evil [one]', is a minor exorcism, as is any prayer which contains a general request to be delivered from the powers of evil. The minor exorcism is a *prayer* to God, while the major exorcism is a *command* to an unclean spirit. The major exorcism will be a very rare event and will be preceded by careful investigation, both spiritual and psychological. It should not be carried out on an individual unless the diocesan bishop has sanctioned it. Since the bishop is not likely to give his permission unless his adviser or deliverance team has investigated the case on his behalf, it is not necessary to give further advice or instruction in this present publication. Bishops or diocesan advisers who require help with any particular case, or wish to consult with other professionals as to appropriate practical or liturgical details, should be in contact with the Christian Exorcism Study Group, who can be approached through the Churches' Council for Health and Healing at St Marylebone Parish Church, Marylebone Road, London NW1 5LT. Others should not consider performing a major exorcism, which is a procedure fraught with dangers both spiritual and physical for the unwary and ill-prepared.

Finally . . .

'Your enemy the devil walketh about, as a roaring lion, seeking whom he may devour' (1 Pet. 5.8). This book has been concerned almost entirely with the Christian ministry of deliverance to disturbed places, disturbed individuals and disturbed families. Let no one be deceived to think otherwise than that this is a minor sphere of the activity of Satan. His great work is to be seen in such obscenities as the nuclear arms race, in the embattled and trustless negotiations between power blocs either internationally or between sections of societies, in apartheid and racial hatreds, in the million and one ways in which humankind behaves as though there were no God in heaven and no heaven for him to be in. Faced with these enormities, it is easy to decry the concerns of this book as being too footling to deserve the time and concern of serious Christians. That would be tragic. Wherever the hand of Satan is to be seen, there the Christian Church must bring the liberating power of the gospel and the message of deliverance. Because there are great areas where Satan holds sway, we are not absolved from doing what we can in the smaller areas. Because he acts upon nations as well as upon individuals, we should not withhold our help, where it can be given, to single persons who need to be delivered from Satan's usurped power. 'These ye should have done, and not left the other undone' (Matt. 23.23). The members of the Christian Exorcism Study Group, and the bishops' advisers in this sphere, believe they have a valid ministry in the name of Christ in his Church, and they ask for the prayers and the understanding of the whole Church as they engage in it. They send forth this volume in the hope that it will increase that understanding and inform those prayers.

Appendix I

The demonic and exorcism in the Bible

In many primitive religions, the world is seen to be crammed full of unseen creatures, some of them good and many of them malevolent. The early religion of Israel was probably no different, seeing the spirit world as a duality of angels and demons. The text of the Old Testament, however, may be interpreted in more than one way on this point. When it speaks (for example) about Lilith or Azazel, does it refer to demons with those names, or is the text about a frightening bird or animal or place? In the dark, when the nightjar's whirring sound sends a chill down your spine, or the jackals are howling, or the sheer emptiness of the trackless desert puts the fear of evil into your soul, it is easy to let the scariness of the situation express itself in terms of alien presences. So how do we translate, for example, Isaiah 34.14? The Revised Standard Version reads:

> The satyr shall cry to his fellow;
> yea, there shall the night hag alight,
> and find for herself a resting place.

A satyr, according to the *Oxford English Dictionary*, is 'one of a class of woodland gods or demons, in form partly human and partly bestial', while the Hebrew word translated 'night hag' is *lilith*, known in later Jewish literature as the first wife of Adam, who flew away and became a demon. When, however, we go to the New English Bible, the verse is far less alarming:

> He-goat shall encounter he-goat.
> There too the nightjar shall rest
> and find herself a place for repose.

Similarly, it is not easy to know who (or what?) Azazel is, in the passage in Leviticus 16 about the scapegoat. When, according to the RSV of Leviticus 16.10, the goat is 'sent away into the wilderness to

Azazel', are we being told about a desert-demon who devours all who are put in his way, or a fallen angel often mentioned in the apocryphal Book of Enoch (6.6 onwards); or is the NEB more likely to be correct when it translates the phrase to refer to the goat being 'driven away into the wilderness to the Precipice'?

Again, the Old Testament has a nice line in vituperation of other cultures and their beliefs when its writers suggest that non-Israelites worship, not the true God, but satyrs or he-goats or demons (look at Lev. 17.7; 2 Kings 23.8; or 2 Chron. 11.13 in various translations). These verses may bear witness to an Israelite belief in demons, but perhaps all we are here witnessing is a picturesque way of making a scornful reference to alien religion, as when English congregations with no great understanding of the comparative study of religion sing that

> The heathen in his blindness
> Bows down to wood and stone.

What is more certain is that as Israelite religion developed, there came to be an increasing belief (especially marked in the writings of Second Isaiah) in the omnipresence and omnipotence of Jahweh as the sole God, bringer of both good and ill. Isaiah 45.6–7 has Jahweh saying

> I am the LORD, there is no other;
> I make the light, I create darkness,
> author alike of prosperity and trouble.

As that idea caught on, what room was there for ideas of demons and spirits who could be blamed for a man's misfortunes? It was one thing to talk of the hosts of heaven, because those were beings who were dependent on Jahweh and who acknowledged his sovereignty; but it was quite another thing to talk about beings who were not of this earth and over whom Jahweh seemed to have no control. Had they not, like the ancient chaos-monster Rahab (Ps. 89.10; Isa. 51.9), been bound by Jahweh, and were they not now powerless and therefore (to all practical intents and purposes) non-existent? Did not the writ of Jahweh extend even over She'ol, death and the demonic (Ps. 139.8 – 'if I make my bed in She'ol, thou art there also')?

That would not quite do. Evil still existed. As Hebrews 2.8 was to say in another context, 'we do not yet see all things in subjection to him'. There had to be an explanation of the evil in nature and the wickedness in man; an explanation which did not compromise the lordship of Jahweh.

The character of the Satan (the word means 'adversary') first appears as the name of a figure in the court of Jahweh, a functionary whom Jahweh allowed to be the agent by which evil happened to good men in order to try them out. The word itself occurs in 1 Samuel 29.14, where the Philistines distrust David and send him back in case 'in the battle he become an adversary (Heb. *satan*) to us' (RSV), or (NEB) 'turn traitor'. Similarly, in the colourful story of Balaam and his ass, the angel of the Lord takes his stand in the way of Balaam 'as his satan' to prevent his going further forward (Num. 22.22). By the time the Book of Job was written, however, 'Satan' has become a named character and when we translate him into English, he deserves a capital letter.

> There was a day when the sons of God came to present themselves before the LORD, and Satan also came among them. The LORD said to Satan, 'Whence have you come? Satan answered the LORD, 'From going to and fro on the earth, and from walking up and down on it'.

The business of Satan as what we may describe as Jahweh's court tester is to send evil to Job in order to see whether his godliness is as disinterested as it seems to be (Job 1.6–12; 2.1–10). It is not long, however, before the Satan begins to get defiled with the pitch he is touching, and his cynicism and eventual opposition to Jahweh begin to show. In Zechariah 3.1 he is certainly less neutral than he was in Job. Joshua the high priest stands before Jahweh's angel, and Satan stands accusing him, but God rebukes him for accusing the innocent. There is an interesting difference between the two accounts of the disastrous census which King David inaugurated. In 2 Samuel 24.1, it is Jahweh who incites David to count the people, but in the account as rewritten by the Chronicler some centuries later (1 Chron. 21.1), 'Satan stood up against Israel, and incited David to number Israel.'

Small wonder that by the time of the New Testament, Satan has become a name of God's archetypal enemy. That is his role throughout the New Testament, from Matthew 4.1 where he tempts Jesus in the wilderness and is told to 'get thee hence', to Revelation 20.2, where 'the dragon, the old serpent, which is the Devil and Satan' is bound and cast into the abyss for a thousand years.

At the centre of the New Testament is the conviction that, in Jesus, the Kingdom of God is coming. Signs of its coming are manifold, but they all boil down to the assertion that we are in the last days, and Satan is meeting his match. Jesus is in the front line of this battle, provoking a head-on clash with Satan, who tempts him personally (Mark 1.13; Luke 4.2; Matt. 4.1); who departs, biding his time (Luke 4.13); whom Jesus has beheld falling from heaven (Luke 10.18); and who musters all his powers at the time of the passion (John 14.30; Luke 22.53), especially by entering into Judas the traitor (Luke 22.3; John 13.27). He wanted to have the whole body of disciples (Luke 22.31), but Jesus prayed that Peter's faith should not fail, and bade him, when he had come to himself, to lend strength to his companions (Luke 22.32).

Satan, also known as Beelzebub or Beelzebul (Matt. 12.24) is the prince of the devils. He has his angels (Matt. 25.41), who seem to be responsible for human disease or illness (Mark 5.8; 9.20). Jesus proves the coming of the Kingdom by giving sight to the blind, making the lame walk, cleansing lepers, letting the deaf hear, raising the dead and proclaiming the good news (Matt. 11.5).

When, however, we move from the Gospels to Paul, we find that his thought is much less demon-centred than that of the Evangelists. Though he writes of 'spiritual hosts of wickedness in high places' (Eph. 6.12), these are principalities, powers, world-rulers of darkness rather than demonic angels of a personal Satan. The great existential reality which opposes God in Paul's thought is sin, which has its power in death (see Romans 6), and it is this which he sees God in Christ confronting and overturning. The way in which Paul sets forth his Gospel with hardly a mention of Satan or of his minions (though we must not underestimate the force of such *obiter dicta* as occur in 1 Cor. 5.5; 2 Cor. 11.4; 1 Thess. 2.18; and elsewhere) leads many present-day Christians to believe that the concept of a personal devil or of demons who may possess a person is a dispensable one for those who want to set forth Christianity to a twentieth-century Western world. They hold that such talk is simply a personification of evil or of disease or dis-ease, a piece of poetic fantasy, a way of speaking which accommodates itself to the superstitions of a long-past world. It is a mistake, they say, to talk of an external devil when some evil is caused by nature, some by disease, and much by the ill-will of evil men and women. Satan is a 'cop-out' from personal responsibility, much as the serpent was for Eve (Gen. 3.13), and as Satan has been for so many since, who say, 'It wasn't me; I don't know what came over me; it must have been an evil spirit who possessed me.'

Some students of the Gospels minimize the elements of exorcism in the ministry of Jesus and conclude that it was not a necessary part of his ministry and need not concern us today. A recent example of this is to be found in an article by Dr J. Keir Howard entitled 'New Testament exorcism and its significance today' in the January 1985 issue of the *Expository Times* (vol. 96, no. 4, pp. 105–9). There are, he admits, numerous references to 'unclean spirits' in the synoptic Gospels, but only six specific cases are recounted. These can mostly be diagnosed in present-day medical terms such as dissociative hysteria, catatonic schizophrenia, or epilepsy. In the Book of Acts, only two cases are told in detail – a possibly mentally handicapped girl supposed to have mediumistic powers (16.16–18), and a schizophrenic or dissociative patient (19.11–17). Exorcism is not mentioned in the fourth Gospel or by Paul, though both refer to demons in a polemical context. 'Paul made mention of the gift of "healing", but there is no thought in any of his writings that this included exorcism' (p. 108).

Dr Howard concludes that in each of the recorded New Testament cases, 'the evidence points to the patient having suffered from some form of mental illness associated with bizarre behaviour patterns or from epilepsy', and, since it is no longer possible for us to view such cases as being induced by the activity of evil spirits, exorcism is no longer appropriate treatment.

> The disordered biochemical mechanisms which lie behind most forms of mental illness are gradually being elucidated, and such conditions should be seen as essentially no different from other manifestations of deranged biochemistry such as diabetes mellitus or an over-active thyroid gland.*

This does not prevent us, in Dr Howard's view, from seeing illness as the work of the prince of evil, but we fight it by medical rather than by exorcistic methods.

Dr Howard is certainly right in warning us against seeing demons in every chapter of the New Testament (or even of the synoptic Gospels), and against the too ready acceptance of 'spirit' language as always inferring an individual or personal agency. It is true that there is biblical warrant for speaking of the spirit of jealousy (Num. 5.14) or the spirit of whoredoms (Hos. 5.4) or the spirit of bondage (Rom. 8.15) or the spirit of fear (2 Tim. 1.7); but there is equal warrant for referring to the spirit of grace (Zech. 12.10) or the spirit of truth (John 14.17) or the spirit of adoption (Rom. 8.15) or the spirit of glory (1 Pet. 4.14). If in these latter cases we see simply a poetic personification of various aspects of the work of God the Holy Spirit, then the former examples should be seen as no more than the descriptions of some of the ways in which Satan goes about his business. As Cardinal Suenens has written:

*Ibid.

No demon of lust was expelled from the adulterous woman (John 8), or from the woman of ill-repute mentioned by Luke (ch. 7), or from the incestuous people of Corinth (1 Cor. 5). No demon of avarice was expelled from Zacchaeus, no demon of incredulity from Peter after his triple betrayal. No demon of rivalry was expelled from the Corinthians whom Paul had to call to order.*

We need to beware of too readily attributing the malaise of troubled souls to the activity of personalized or individual spirits whom we attempt to cast out under the name of 'the spirit of insanity' or 'the spirit of murder'. The scriptural arguments for doing so are very shaky.

On the other hand, if we believe in the existence of God and of Satan and of human beings (both incarnate in this world and discarnate or re-embodied in another form in another world or worlds), there is no reason in logic why there should not be a great Chain of Being which includes all sorts of creatures and spiritual beings like angels and demons, and why some of them should not owe allegiance to God and work for good, while others of them belong to Satan and influence us to do evil. Nor is there any reason why some forms of dis-ease should not be open to treatment at the same time on the medical, the psychiatric *and* the spiritual level. Health and wholeness is the will of God for all creation, and any interference with that will is to be seen as the work of Satan. God is the creator of the totality of man in his bodily, mental and spiritual aspects, and Satan will seek to destroy health or wholeness – in body, in mind and in spirit. That is not to say that all sickness is a reward for sin. If it were so, then Satan would be working in a clear and logical way, which is not his wont. Nor is it to say that Christians cannot use even physical suffering as a means towards spiritual growth, for nothing is so evil as to be completely irredeemable by grace. What it does imply is that in the irrationality of sickness we see the irrationality of Satan, who sometimes attacks in a purely physical way – in which case he is to be counteracted by purely physical medicine – and sometimes in other ways, when the appropriate treatments will be upon another level.

In practice, of course, few maladies are purely somatic. Most are psychosomatic in varying degrees, and Christians will also believe that they can be pneumatosomatic – that is, that they need to be treated at a spiritual level as well as at bodily and mental levels. There are times when that spiritual level should very definitely *not* be particularized as an external 'demon'; to externalize the malady in that way may be a great

Renewal and the Powers of Darkness. Darton, Longman and Todd (1983), p. 17.

'cop-out' which prevents healing being accomplished on the spiritual level at all, because it removes the cause of the malady from the responsibility of the patient instead of making him confront his own spiritual poverty and determine to do something about it. But there may well be times when that diagnosis which talks of direct demonic involvement ought to be considered. The important thing is to treat the patient as a whole person, and not to sectionalize him. It is a very unhelpful kind of medicine that *only* sees 'a case of catatonic schizophrenia' rather than a whole person who is dis-eased and who needs treatment at a medical, a mental and a spiritual level. Had the Gerasene demoniac (Mark 5.1–13) been treated as a case of catatonic schizophrenia and nothing else, the demon which had used the schizophrenic state in order to gain entrance to, and possession of, his personality, would have found a swept and garnished room all ready for a worse invasion to follow (Matt. 12.44).

There are cases which need spiritual as well as psychiatric treatment, and both the priest who is tempted to work without the psychiatrist and the doctor who has no time for the priest may need to take to heart the words of Matthew 23.13 – 'these you ought to have done, without neglecting the other'. Both/and is often a better medicine than either/or. That is certainly the attitude inculcated in Ecclesiasticus 38, where both spiritual and medical means are commended to the sufferer:

> My son, if you have an illness, do not neglect it,
> but pray to the Lord, and he will heal you.
> Renounce your faults, amend your ways,
> and cleanse your heart from all sin.
> Bring a savoury offering and bring flour for a token
> and pour oil on the sacrifice; be as generous as you can.
> Then call in the doctor, for the Lord created him;
> do not let him leave you, for you need him (Ecclus 38.9–12).

Although there may be only a small number of specific accounts of exorcism in the synoptic Gospels and in Acts, belief in the existence both of good angels and of evil spirits is pervasive. There were angels who ministered to Jesus after his temptation (Mark 1.13) and at the Garden of Gethsemane (Luke 22.43) and who would, if bidden, have descended in their thousands to rescue him from the cross (Matt. 26.53). There are the guardian angels of little children (Matt. 18.10) and the messengers who heralded the birth and the resurrection of Jesus (Luke 2.13; Matt. 28.2–7).

As with angels, so with demons. Both Jesus and his followers acted as though there existed, not only Satan himself, but lesser beings who were part of his rule. The man of Gerasa whom Jesus healed (Mark 5) had an 'unclean spirit' so divisive and fissiparous that it was named Legion, and it was hard to know whether to address it (them?) in the singular or the plural. Mary Magdalene had had to be cleansed of seven devils (Luke 8.2), and a single demon cast out of a man can come back with seven other worse spirits and take up residence again, if the space they find is empty, swept and garnished (Matt. 12.43–5). After the resurrection, the followers of Jesus not only challenged the rule of Satan by proclaiming the Kingdom of God in the name of Jesus, they also cast out the devils who were the continuing sign of Satan's misappropriated lordship over the sons of men (see Mark 16.17; Acts 5.6; 19.12ff.). They did this because they believed it was the will and command of Jesus that they should so do (Matt. 10.8; Luke 9.1; and the – later – ending of Mark's Gospel in Mark 16.17).

It needs to be pointed out, however, that not all the healings attributed to Jesus, and not all those chronicled in the Acts of the Apostles, were dealt with in terms of demonic activity. That 'demons' were only one of a number of possible diagnoses of illness is clear from Matthew 4.24, where it is reported that among those who were brought to Jesus and cured were 'sufferers from every kind of illness, racked with pain, possessed by devils, epileptic, or paralysed'. There was need for judgement and discrimination, whereby a person's case had to be looked at as a whole, and a decision reached as to whether this was a case for exorcism or for some other kind of treatment. It simply is not true that any and every kind of illness was in those days miscategorized as demonic possession. In his book *Christ Triumphant*,* Dr Graham Twelftree examines the world of thought contemporary with Jesus of Nazareth, particularly in Philo and Josephus, and concludes that they

> were not uncritical in their acceptance of a report of a miracle . . . Not everyone believed in demons and exorcism . . . People in the New Testament world [were able] to discriminate between those sicknesses which were and those which were not thought to be caused by demons.

That, presumably, is why cases which look to us to be virtually identical were treated in different ways. Compare, for example, the cures of deaf, dumb and blind persons in Mark 7.32–7 and 8.22–5, where there is no

*Hodder and Stoughton (1985), p. 169.

question of exorcism (despite Mark's interest in exorcism stories in 5.1–10; 7.24–30; 9.14–29; and elsewhere) with the very similar cases in Matthew 9.32 and 12.22, where dumb and blind persons are exorcized. There must have been some diagnosis or discernment by Jesus at the time, whereby he was able to tell which cases required the casting-out of evil spirits and which did not. Dr Twelftree co-authored a study on this point with Professor J. D. G. Dunn, which was published in *Churchman*, vol. 94, no. 3 (1980) under the title 'Demon-Possession and Exorcism in the New Testament', and which concluded that

> by no means all illnesses were attributed to demons and demon-possession. There were well-established maladies like fever, leprosy and paralysis which it was not thought necessary to attribute either to Satan or to demons (Mark 1:29–31, 40–4, 2:1–12; cf. Mark 4:19). There were conditions which could be attributed to Satan, either because the cause was inexplicable or as a particular manifestation of Satan's rule over this age (Luke 13:16; Acts 10:38; cf. Mark 4:15; Matthew 13:39). But the idea of demon-possession was reserved for conditions where the individual seemed to be totally in the grip of an evil power (using his vocal cords, Mark 1:24, 5:7, 9; Acts 16:16; convulsing him, Mark 1:26, 9:20–2, 26; superhuman strength, Mark 5:3–4; Acts 19:16).*

Dr Twelftree's *Christ Triumphant* may be commended as the most thorough and recent treatment of exorcism, both in its New Testament form and as practised in certain sections of the Christian Church today. His reading of the New Testament evidence reaches a very different conclusion from that of Dr Howard. Jesus was certainly an exorcist, like others of his time, but 'we cannot claim that exorcism was *the* key to his ministry; simply with Matthew 12:28/Luke 11:20 in mind, that exorcism was at least one of the important functions or aspects of his ministry' (pp. 78–9). The different strands of the New Testament writings bear witness to different emphases in different first-century congregations. The Johannine churches probably had less to do with exorcism than those under Lucan influence, but not even Luke permits us 'to take exorcism as in any way the most important part of the Church's ministry' (p. 107). It is, however, 'reasonable to suppose that Jesus intended his disciples to continue their preaching and exorcisms until the complete coming of the Kingdom' (p. 85), and the early Church continued this

*Art. cit., p. 217.

practice after Easter, at which stage, 'rather than being peripheral to the ministry, the early Christians accepted exorcism as an important part of their mission' in some (if not all) of the first-century churches (p. 132).

How did Jesus diagnose the need for exorcism, and how did he perform it? According to Dr Twelftree,

(a)   In the story of the Gadarene demoniac, extraordinary strength (Mark 5:3f) and a disregard for pain (5:5) are mentioned. With this can be compared the violence associated with the suffering of the boy in Mark 9:22.

(b)   In three stories in Mark (1:24, 5:7 and 9:14) the demoniacs are disturbed when confronted with Jesus, and in the first two mentioned, the demoniacs vocalize their distress.

(c)   In Mark 1:24f and 5:8ff the demons are said to speak. From history of religious parallels . . . we can at least say that the voice of the sufferer was thought to be affected.

Thus from the Gospel accounts we can suggest that it may have been on these grounds that Jesus identified the need for an exorcism.*

As to the method of exorcism, 'Jesus seems to have been a man of his time in that he used readily recognizable techniques, and what was reported of other exorcists was also reported of Jesus' exorcisms' (Twelftree, p. 70). His words were simple and straightforward. On occasions he asked the name of the demon (Mark 5.9); his incantations are reported as 'Be bound, and come out of him' (Mark 1.25), and 'Come out of him and no longer enter into him' (Mark 9.25) which are, according to Twelftree, part of 'a readily recognizable stock of incantational formulae' (p. 66). However, Jesus appears to have used no mechanical devices such as the incense of Tobit 8.3 or the amulets of his contemporaries; he is not recorded as praying when he performed an exorcism; and he did not call up or invoke any power-authority. It seems as if 'Jesus deliberately draws attention to himself and his own resources in his ability to expel the demon' (p. 70).

In the early Church, by contrast, exorcists did not act on their own authority, but invoked the authority of Jesus (for example, 'I charge you in the name of Jesus Christ to come out of her' – Acts 16.18). The itinerant Jewish exorcists used the formula, 'I adjure you by the Jesus whom Paul preaches' (Acts 19.13), though the sons of Sceva got their

*Op. cit., p. 71.

come-uppance for using this formula without being true followers of him of whose name they were making use.

To summarize: Exorcism was common in the world of our Lord's day, and Jesus was himself an exorcist. He seems to have discriminated between cases in which exorcism was appropriate and those where it was not. Exorcism was certainly practised by the earliest Christians, though probably it was more highly valued in some congregations than in others.

Appendix I I

The Christian tradition of exorcism

The practice of exorcism has continued in the Christian Church right down to our own day, but it has taken different forms at different times and in different communions. Much of our evidence for the practice in patristic times is of a liturgical nature and relates to Christian initiation. The devil is seen to be particularly active in the non-Christian world and therefore all that comes into the Church needs to be purified from his taint. It is not necessarily that non-Christians are thought to be possessed by Satan or his demons, but the world outside the Church is so affected by the all-pervasive effect of Satan's rule that there is need for disinfestation to be very thoroughly carried out before a convert can be regarded as safely within the Christian household.

The earliest surviving mentions of exorcisms in relation to Christian initiation are those of Rome in the early third century, preserved in the *Apostolic Tradition* of Hippolytus. Candidates were exorcized by their sponsors, at the end of each weekly instruction by their teacher and immediately before baptism by the bishop. So creation was liberated from the disorder and distortions of Satan by the action of Jesus Christ in his Church.

The Orthodox Churches of the East preserve this practice, and exorcism is primarily connected with the rite of baptism. In the first part of the rite, the 'Making of a Catechumen', there are three prayers of exorcism directed against the devil, commanding him to 'be afraid, and depart, and absent yourself from this creature, and come not back . . . but get you hence to your own Tartarus, until the appointed day of judgement'. At the end of the three exorcisms there is a prayer that the eyes of the catechumen may be open to the illumination of the gospel, after which the priest breathes on him, saying, 'Drive out from him every evil and unclean spirit, hiding and lurking in his heart.' It will be seen, therefore, that there are both prayers to God and commands to evil entities; but it would be false to suggest that in this context one could be described as a minor and the other as a major exorcism.

In the *Mega* and *Mikron Euchologion* of the Greek Church there are prayers of exorcism for various other occasions. The current *Mikron Euchologion* of the Apostolic Diaconate Publications of the Church of Greece contains three prayers by St Basil the Great and four by St John Chrysostom for those who are demon-possessed or possessed by sickness, as well as Prayers of the Lance (said by the priest, who crosses people with the lance which is used for cutting the communion bread) and prayers against the *baskania*, or 'evil eye'. There is no separate order of exorcists in the Eastern Church, and exorcism against the evil eye is performed by 'charismatic' lay people (male or female) or monastics who are popularly recognized as being able to perform such a function.

By contrast, the Church of the West regularized exorcism by making the second of the minor orders that of 'exorcist', an office which is first attested in the time of Pope Cornelius in the mid-third century, and which was retained within the Roman Catholic Church until the reforms of the ordinal which took place in the 1960s. Even when the office existed, however, its functions were purely vestigial; the future priest was told that he received the power to exorcize, but that the actual function of that power was reserved to the bishop or his mandatory.

Minor exorcism, that is a prayer to God in the name of Christ, directed against the powers of evil, can be carried out by any baptized Christian (or even by an unbeliever). The mere use of the Lord's Prayer with its petition 'deliver us from [the] evil [one]', is a form of minor exorcism, and there are many forms of 'breastplate' prayer, of which perhaps the best-known is that attributed to St Patrick. These are, technically, self-administered minor exorcisms used by lay Christians in situations of danger or temptation. But since it is always advisable to follow every exorcism with a blessing, on the principle of not leaving the house empty (Matt. 12.44-5), it is logical to have a priest present for a formal exorcism, even a minor one.

The Roman baptismal rite still contains prayers for the exorcism of the candidate, and exorcisms are still prescribed in connection with the preparation of holy water, for the blessing of the baptismal font, for the materials to be used for holy unction, on sites where churches are to be consecrated, and elsewhere. These prayers may be used by any priest, but when a case of possession has been diagnosed and there is need for the 'greater exorcism', the form laid down in the *Rituale Romanum* is used, and this can only be done by a priest specially and explicitly authorized by the diocesan bishop to do so.

In the Churches of the Reformation, there is a variety of attitudes towards the practice of exorcism. Some Christians, especially of the charismatic persuasion, are apt to see the activity of demons in everything that runs counter to their own understanding of the Christian religion. This can sometimes lead to bizarre and tragic occurrences such as the notorious 'Barnsley' case (see *The Times* for 26 and 27 March 1975) in which a husband murdered his wife after an all-night exorcism during which a group of charismatic Christians claimed to have exorcized many demons from him, but failed to remove the demon of murder. A later case (reported in *The Times* for 4 September 1980) involved a preacher and his friend who kicked a mentally unstable woman to death as they tried to rid her of the evil spirit, allegedly that of Judas Iscariot, which was possessing her. The cases in 1975 led a number of Churches to seek to clarify their stance towards the question of exorcism.

The Methodist Conference of 1976 approved a 'Statement on Exorcism' which may be obtained from the Methodist Church Division of Social Responsibility. Exorcism, it said, is an allowable ingredient within total pastoral care, occasionally applicable. But it is only one aspect among others, and total pastoral care will involve a multi-disciplinary approach. Ministers should avail themselves of this option only after consultation with their superintendent minister or chairman of district, after a thorough pastoral investigation and in close collaboration with suitable persons qualified in medicine, psychology and the social services. There should be continuing aftercare.

At about the same time, the General Assembly of the Church of Scotland received a 'Report of the Working Party on Parapsychology' (21 May 1976). The Working Party had been set up in 1974 to examine 'recent experiments in the field of Parapsychology', but in the following year 'the vexed question of exorcism' was added to its remit. The Working Party concluded that

> such a ceremonial as Exorcism does more harm than good by its existence within the practice of the Church. We believe that it effects nothing that cannot be accomplished by the expeditious use of medical skills and pastoral skills . . . There is no place in the Reformed Scottish tradition for such a rite to be devised . . . Any person encountering a case of alleged 'possession' should refer it to a physician.*

The position in the Church of England is in practice very similar to that in the Roman Catholic Church. The Canons of 1603/4 laid down that

*Paragraphs 36, 45 and 51.

no minister or ministers shall without the licence and direction of the Bishop of the Diocese first obtained and had under his hand and seal ... attempt upon any pretence whatsoever, either of possession or obsession, by fasting and prayer to cast out any devil or devils, under pain of the imputation of imposture, or cousenage,* and deposition from the Ministry (Canon 72).

This provision was repealed in 1969 together with the bulk of the Canons of 1603/4, and no canonical rule has replaced it, although there remain vestiges of the practice of minor exorcism. For example, in the Baptism service of the Alternative Service Book 1980, the traditional rite of the making of a catechumen has been partly restored. The renunciation of evil is followed by the giving of the sign of the cross and a minor exorcism in the words, 'May almighty God deliver you from the powers of darkness, and lead you in the light and obedience of Christ' (p. 230).

In 1972, a Commission appointed by the then Bishop of Exeter, and containing Roman Catholic as well as Anglican members, issued its report entitled *Exorcism* (edited by Dom Robert Petitpierre OSB). Among its recommendations was that 'it is much to be desired that every diocesan bishop should appoint a priest as diocesan exorcist, and that in each province centres of training should be established'. Movement towards this goal was slow and patchy until the unhappy events of 1975 gave impetus to it. In that year, the House of Bishops laid down guidelines in the form of an answer to a question asked at General Synod (see the *Report of Proceedings*, vol. 6, no. 2 (July 1975), p. 361). The ruling was that

there are many men and women so within the grip of the power of evil that they need the aid of the Christian Church in delivering them from it. When this ministry is carried out the following factors should be borne in mind:

1 It should be done in collaboration with the resources of medicine.

2 It should be done in the context of prayer and sacrament.

3 It should be done with the minimum of publicity.

4 It should be done by experienced persons authorized by the diocesan bishop.

5 It should be followed up by continuing pastoral care.

*Now spelt – if the word is used at all – cozenage. It is defined by the *OED* as 'the practice of deception'.

By the mid-1980s, the vast majority of English dioceses had priests described variously as 'diocesan exorcist', 'diocesan adviser on the paranormal', 'bishop's adviser on psychic and occult phenomena', etc. The trend today is to have a 'bishop's team for the ministry of deliverance' rather than to rely on an isolated individual. These teams often have a psychiatrist member, and usually spend most of their time giving advice to parish clergymen, rather than themselves engaging in the appropriate liturgical and pastoral functions. In accordance with the fourth of the bishops' guidelines above, however, it would be unusual for a major exorcism of a person to be carried out without at least one member of the diocesan team being present. Advice for diocesan teams is given in Appendix III. It has been drawn up by the Christian Exorcism Study Group, which continues the work of the 'Exeter' Commission, and has, over the years, sought to develop lines along which the practices of exorcism might be responsibly exercised.

At the regular residential conferences of the Group, training is offered to diocesan advisers and members of bishop's teams. Group members have also lectured at in-service training events for the clergy in some dioceses, led courses in theological colleges and spoken to clergy chapters and similar gatherings. Over the years since the 'Exeter Report', norms of diagnosis and treatment have gradually evolved. This present volume represents the result of a convergence of viewpoint and practice which has been established within the Group over the years.

Appendix III

The diocese: teamwork and network

In reply to a question asked of the House of Bishops in General Synod on 30 June 1975, Archbishop Donald Coggan said that the ministry of deliverance 'should be done by experienced persons authorized by the diocesan bishop'. Nearly every diocesan bishop in the Church of England has now given such authorization, some to an individual priest, but in an increasing number of cases to a team including clerical and lay members.

The bishop needs to ensure that his clergy and accredited lay ministers know of the existence of this team and how to make contact with it, but this must be done in a discreet way and without publicity beyond the circle of people needing to have this information. Sometimes this is done by publicizing the telephone number of the bishop's office or bishop's chaplain, or of the relevant rural dean, so that a 'neutral' person can filter inquiries through to the team. Sometimes the name and telephone number of the team convener is published in an *Ad clerum* or in the diocesan directory of information.

The reason for restricting this kind of information is that if too much publicity is given to the identity of members of the diocesan deliverance team, they are in danger of being overexposed to importunacy and/or harassed by members of the occult or Satanist fraternities. What is of equal import is that a public stress on the ministry of the team may lead to the ministry of the parish priest being underplayed. The normal channel of approach on behalf of a troubled person should be for the parish priest to seek the advice of the team. Clients ought not to contact the team members direct. The team should be seen as supplementing, strengthening and upbuilding the pastoral and priestly work of the parish clergy, and not as supplanting it. Their normal function should be to be told of cases which have come the way of the parish clergyman, to discuss them with him either over the telephone or by meeting, and to advise him how best to handle the case in question. As far as the client is concerned (in the vast majority of cases) the team will only be an anonymous 'second opinion' sought by the parish priest in order to satisfy himself that he is working along the right lines. Only in exceptional cases will the team take over the client from the parish priest, and then only for the 'critical phase'. The continuing pastoral care and long-term incorporation within a worshipping Christian community can only be done by the clergyman and congregation on the spot.

A diocesan team should ideally consist of a number of priests, at least one psychiatrist, and at least one woman. The non-medical members *must* be Christians, though it is possible to work with agnostic or even atheist psychiatrists, providing they are sufficiently in sympathy with the aims and methods of the group not to be a destructive force within it.

There may well be a penumbra to the group, consisting of medical or psychiatric experts whose advice may be sought from time to time. It is also useful to have people available who can act as observers or recorders; and if there can in addition be a priest in each deanery who has been trained in elementary diagnosis, he can save the team a great deal of time and trouble by dealing with simple cases, weeding out obvious cases of mental disturbance, amd preparing reports for the team on cases which need their expert advice.

The group should meet three or four times a year to review cases which have been presented to members. This will ensure that the group members are all working along more or less the same lines, that they have the benefit of knowing about a wide variety of cases so that their own diagnostic skills can be continually developed, and that they get to know each other's strengths and weaknesses. This last point is important as it helps a team member know to whom to refer a case with which (for whatever reason) he cannot deal in person.

If there is to be a major exorcism of a person, the group will have to obtain the bishop's permission before proceeding, so that the bishop will know at least that much about the group's activities. It is also much to be desired that the group make an annual report to the bishop, either in writing or by interview, so that he is au fait with what its members are doing in his name.

Team members need ongoing training. To some extent this will be provided by periodic case conferences at the regular meetings of the team, but it is fatally easy for isolated teams to become at least idiosyncratic and even misguided. The annual conference of the Christian Exorcism Study Group is a useful opportunity for mutual support, mutual criticism and mutual training. It is much to be hoped that every member of a diocesan team should attend this conference from time to time.

The ministry of deliverance should not be an esoteric ministry understood by only one or two people within a diocese. The more widely it is understood and appreciated by the parish clergy, the better. Some theological colleges include courses on this ministry as part of the pastoral training for their ordinands. Would that all of them did so! Diocesan teams should also take every opportunity of including the ministry of deliverance as the subject for regular seminars in in-service training for the clergy in their diocese. Again, the Christian Exorcism Study Group is ready to advise and (on occasion) to provide seminar leaders for this purpose.

In the 'normal' case, then, where the parish priest is confronted by a client for whom he suspects the ministry of deliverance might be indicated, or in a case where the occult, psychic or ostensibly paranormal aspects with which he is presented make him feel 'out of his depth', the system might work as follows:

1   The parish priest contacts the team in the way appropriate in his particular diocese – direct; by way of the rural dean; by way of the bishop's office, etc.

2   The team member who has received the initial approach will counsel the parish priest to the best of his ability, either over the telephone or by a visit. He will make notes of the details and of advice given. Most cases will be dealt with in this way, with the parish priest reporting the outcome of his visits to the disturbed house or client and receiving ongoing advice as the case proceeds. The team member may very well consult with his colleagues if there are unusual or difficult aspects of the case.

3   If the team thinks the case warrants it, they may ask an experienced priest to visit the client and report back. Should there be a prima facie case for exorcism either of place or person, *at least two team members* should see the client – in his own home, not in the home of a team member – and accompanied by the parish priest who has referred the case.

4   A provisional diagnosis is arrived at, and detailed notes are taken. This report will be studied by the team, and a corporate decision arrived at. Perhaps the conclusion will be that there is no case; or that there is a case, but that it requires other treatment than exorcism – blessing, laying-on of hands, prayer, a Eucharist, or an explanation to the client of the psychodynamics of a fraught household.

5   If the team decides that there needs to be an exorcism of a place, it will probably proceed immediately. Should, however, the decision be for the greater exorcism, i.e. of a person, this should never be carried out until a competent psychiatric opinion has been obtained and the express permission of the bishop has been granted.

6   In all cases of greater (or major) exorcism, a written report should be submitted to the bishop as soon as possible after it has taken place. This may be supplemented by 'progress reports' of the case at later stages if anything of significance happens.

The necessity of having professional psychiatric opinion available within the diocesan team raises the question of the proper collaboration of priest and psychiatrist. It is difficult to lay down a precise code of practice, but the following points are important and deserve emphasis:

1   Each discipline should approach the other with respect and professional and ethical dignity.

2   The priest and doctor should consult each other concerning their respective codes of confidentiality. The priest should reassure the doctor that high standards of confidentiality are to be maintained, and that the strict code of practice required of the priest is enshrined in Canon Law.

3   The priest should inform the doctor that he has been called to see one of his patients. In return, the doctor should seek the advice of the patient's priest at an early stage where paranormal phenomena or experience is suspected. The permission of the patient must be sought for such cross-referral in each case, and there should be no cross-referral if the patient does not wish there to be – whatever the opinion of the priest or doctor about its advisability.

4   It is useful to reassure the doctor that although there is a wide variety of opinion among the clergy, there is in nearly every diocese a team of persons who have the expertise, who have been appointed to this ministry by the bishop, and who may be called upon for advice. It might also be useful for the doctor to know that there are also psychiatrists expert in this field who may be contacted.

5   Following investigation and treatment by the parish priest with advice from the specialist team (and in some cases the team's direct involvement), proper aftercare should be arranged between the patient's parish priest and general practitioner.

6   It is perfectly possible for the priest involved in this ministry to work with a psychiatrist who is an agnostic, provided that each accepts the disciplines and valid experience of the other, and that the priest accepts that the doctor has the over-riding legal responsibility for the welfare of the patient. In some circumstances, a working relationship may be possible with an atheist psychiatrist, though this will probably present obvious difficulties in relation to the spiritual care of the patient. The supreme factor is that there shall be a desire and acceptance on both sides that they are each concerned with the same ultimate aim – to restore the patient to wholeness.

7   In the training of priests and psychiatrists, there should be the opportunity for learning about each other's methods and disciplines. Both at theological college and at medical school, students should understand more about psychology and pastoral care, so that doctors and priests will increasingly come to regard each other as co-professionals. This education should continue into professional life, so that a psychiatrist should not think it unusual to seek the advice of a priest when he appreciates that the signs and symptoms of a particular case are alien to his own discipline. In hospital cases, the hospital chaplain should be involved as part of the consultative structure.

8   As the nature of the ministry of deliverance is widely misunderstood among psychiatrists and Christians alike, a great deal of education, dialogue and mutual support is required. It is desirable to establish the sort of relationships where personal rapport can lead to a growing sense of mutual confidence at a human level, to enable people trained in different disciplines to work together for the patient's benefit.

Appendix IV

Liturgical and prayer material

The material which follows must not be treated as though it were a magical incantation whose effectiveness depends upon its exact verbal repetition. What matters is that the will of the person who is praying and acting should be in union with the will of God in Christ through his Holy Spirit, and that there should be a pure intention to work as an agent of Christ's Church in making God's will effective in his world. It is for the person who uses this material to decide how much or how little of it he takes, and whether to use the prayers as they are given here or to express their sentiments in his own words.

A great deal of this Appendix (namely, sections I V, V, V I I, I X and X) is taken, with permission, from the draft report made by the Liturgical Committee of the Church of the Province of South Africa in October 1983. We are grateful to them for allowing us to use their (so far unpublished) material in this way.

I

THE BLESSING OF A HOUSE

In the Name of the Father, and of the Son, and of the Holy Spirit:

As it was in the beginning, is now, and ever shall be, world without end. Amen.

At the entrance

Peace be to this house:

And to all who dwell in it.

Let us pray:
Lord, you gave to your Church authority to act in your Name. We ask you therefore to visit today what we visit, and to bless whatever we bless;

120

and grant that as we enter this house in lowliness of heart, all powers of evil may be put to flight and the angel of peace may enter in. Defend from harm all who enter and leave this door, and give your protection to the members of this household in their going out and in their coming in; through Jesus Christ our Lord. *Amen.*

The Gospel

Luke 19.1–10

Blessing of water for sprinkling in the rooms

Blessed are you, Lord, God of all creation; through your goodness we have this salt and water to be hallowed by the invocation of your holy Name. As salt was made by the Lord's word to be the symbol of his disciples in the world, and as water was consecrated for the rebirth of his people in baptism, so we mix this salt and water in the Name of ✠ the Father and of ✠ the Son and of ✠ the Holy Spirit; and we pray that wherever it is sprinkled, all evil may be banished and your blessing may abide there; through Jesus Christ our Lord. *Amen.*

In a bedroom

Lord God our heavenly Father, you neither slumber nor sleep. Bless the bedrooms of this house and guard with your continual watchfulness all who take rest within these walls, that refreshed by the gift of sleep they may wake to serve you joyfully in their daily work; through Jesus Christ our Lord. *Amen.*

In a child's room

Almighty God our heavenly Father, your blessed Son at Nazareth shared the life of an earthly home. Bless all children who shall live in this house and grant wisdom and understanding to all who have care of them, that they may grow up in your constant fear and love; through Jesus Christ our Lord. *Amen.*

In the kitchen

Grant, Lord, to all who shall work in this room that in serving others they may serve you and share in your perfect service, and that in the busyness of the kitchen they may possess you in tranquillity; through Jesus Christ our Lord. *Amen.*

At the dining table

Lord God, you give good things liberally and without stint. Grant that all who shall eat and drink together at this table may be joined in true friendship and may praise you with thankful hearts; through Jesus Christ our Lord. *Amen.*

In the study

Lord, you are the true Light that lightens every man that comes into the world. Bless this place of study, that those who come here may come to the knowledge of your will, and daily increase in spiritual understanding of the love and glory of the one true God who lives and reigns, Father, Son and Holy Spirit, world without end. *Amen.*

In the living room

Lord God, your blessed Son has said, Henceforth I have called you friends. Unite in true friendship and love all who shall meet in this room; through Jesus Christ our Lord. *Amen.*

Our Father in heaven,
hallowed be your name,
your kingdom come,
your will be done,
on earth as in heaven.
Give us today our daily bread.
Forgive us our sins
as we forgive those who sin against us.
Lead us not into temptation
but deliver us from evil.
For the kingdom, the power and the glory are yours
now and for ever. *Amen.*

The blessing of the house

Lord God, holy, blessed and glorious Trinity, ✠ bless, ✠ hallow and

✠ sanctify this house that in it there may be joy and gladness, peace and love, health and goodness, and thanksgiving always to you, Father, Son and Holy Spirit; and let your blessing rest upon this house and those who dwell in it, now and for ever. *Amen.*

To God alone be the glory for ever and ever. *Amen.*

II

HOLY COMMUNION AT THE BLESSING OF A HOUSE OR HOME

Introductory sentence

Unless the Lord builds the house, its builders will have toiled in vain (Ps. 127.1).

Collect

Visit, Lord, we pray, this house, and drive from it all the snares of the enemy. Let your holy angels dwell here to keep us in peace, and may your blessing be upon it evermore; through Jesus Christ our Lord. *Amen.*

Epistle

Philippians 4.4–8

Gospel

Luke 19.1–10

Postcommunion sentence

Jesus said, 'Anyone who loves me will heed what I say; then my Father will love him, and we will come to him and make our home with him' (John 14.23).

III

REQUIEM EUCHARIST

The prayers provided in the *Alternative Service Book 1980* for the Commemoration of the Faithful Departed (pp. 834–7) are suitable. Some of the prayers in the Funeral section of the ASB are also appropriate, particularly prayer 12 on page 315, the Collect on page 331, and some of the 'Selection of Additional Prayers' on pages 334–6.

IV

THE RITE OF EXORCISM OF A HOME OR OTHER PLACE
(South African)

In the Name of God, Father, Son and Holy Spirit.

Amen.

Lord, have mercy.

Lord, have mercy.

Christ, have mercy.

Christ, have mercy.

Lord, have mercy.

Lord, have mercy.

Let us pray.
All praise to you, almighty Father; you have overcome him who has the power of death. Strengthen us by your Spirit and make us worthy to perform rightly the blessing of this home (place). Let all evil spirits be put to flight and may the angel of peace enter in; in the Name of Jesus Christ our Lord. *Amen.*

The earth is the Lord's and all that is in it.

The world and those who dwell therein.

In the faith of Christ Jesus we claim this place for God, Father, Son and Holy Spirit. *Amen.*

Any of the following prayers may be used, especially in parts of the house where they seem most desirable. Other similar prayers may be needed, and prayer should continue, either aloud or in silence, until the place is delivered.

In your love, O Lord, enter this place which is part of your dominion. As you make your home in the hearts of your faithful people, grant also that in this home (place) your presence may be known and that the evil spirits be banished for ever. We ask this through Christ our Lord. *Amen.*

Almighty and eternal God, you are present in every part of your creation. Protect this home (place) and let no evil here oppose your rule. But grant that by the merit of the holy cross and the power of your Holy Spirit, your people may serve you, free from fear; through Jesus Christ our Lord. *Amen.*

Lord Jesus Christ, at a word you drove out demons and by your power vanquished Satan. Give us, who call in faith upon your Name, the confidence and strength to drive the evil one from this place; for you alone are our defence, you alone our Lord. *Amen.*

Creator of all things visible and invisible, you are God alone and there is none beside you. Your Kingdom is everlasting and your power infinite; we beseech you to free your servants in this place from all the might of wicked spirits and from all their terrors and deceptions. Guard them and keep them safe for ever, through Jesus Christ our Lord. *Amen.*

Deliver us, merciful Lord, from all evils, past, present and to come, and grant us peace in our day. Keep us free from sin and safe from all distress as we wait in joyful hope for the coming of our Saviour, Jesus Christ. *Amen.*

Free this place, O Lord, from all disturbances of demons and deliver it from every manifestation of the evil one; through Christ, the conqueror of sin. *Amen.*

The following adjuration may be necessary:

Be gone from this place, every evil haunting and phantasm;
Depart for ever, every unclean spirit;
Be banished, every delusion and deceit of Satan;

Be put to flight, every evil power.
In the Name of the living God.
In the Name of the holy God.
In the Name of the God of all creation.
In the Name of Jesus Christ his only Son, and in the power of his Holy Spirit. *Amen.*

In the Name of God, Father, Son and Holy Spirit: we order you, every evil spirit, to leave this place, harming no one, and to go to the place appointed you. *Amen.*

At the end, one or both of the following are always said:

O Lord, holy Father, almighty and eternal God: hear our prayer, and send forth from heaven your holy angels to watch over and protect all who live within this house (place); through Jesus Christ our Lord. *Amen.*

Visit, we beseech you, O Lord, this home, and drive far from it all the snares of the evil one. Let your holy angels dwell here to preserve us in peace, and may your blessing be upon us evermore. *Amen.*

Those living in the place may be personally blessed with laying-on of hands.

May our Lord Jesus Christ himself, and God our Father, who loved us and in his grace has given us unfailing courage and a firm hope, encourage and comfort you, that you may always do and say what is good. May the Lord who is faithful strengthen you, and keep you safe from the evil one. And now may the Lord of peace himself give you peace at all times and in every way. *Amen.* (2 Thess. 2.16–17; 3.3–5, 16.)

And the blessing of God Almighty, the Father, the Son and the Holy Ghost, be among you and remain with you always. *Amen.*

V

FORM FOR THE BLESSING OF HOLY WATER
(South African)

If the water is to be blessed at the beginning of a service for the exorcism of a home or other place, all three following prayers are used. Otherwise the second and third will suffice.

We come to bless this home (place) and pray that the presence of God may be known and felt in it, that all that is evil and unclean may be driven far from it. As a sign of the pouring forth and cleansing of God's Holy Spirit which we desire for this home (place), we use this water. Water has been ordained by Christ for use in the sacrament of baptism. So let us pray that God will bless this water.

Then, indicating the water, the priest says:

Lord God Almighty, the Creator of life, we ask you to bless this water. As in faith we shall use it, forgive us our sins, support us in sickness, and protect us from the power of evil. In your mercy, Lord, give us that living water which becomes a spring welling up to eternal life. Guard us in every danger and bring us at the last into the fullness of your presence. We ask this through Christ our Lord. *Amen.*

Salt may be used and mixed with the water:

Almighty God, we ask you to bless this salt as once you blessed the salt scattered by the prophet Elisha over the water. Wherever this salt and water are sprinkled, drive away the power of the evil one and always protect us by the presence of your Holy Spirit. Grant this through Christ our Lord. *Amen.*

VI

BLESSING AND HEALING OF PERSONS

Forms for the blessing of persons, with laying-on of hands and anointing and Holy Communion, may be found in *Ministry to the Sick*, as authorized by the General Synod of the Church of England in 1983 and available on card or in booklet form (booklet ASB 70; card ASB 71). If appropriate, the form may be preceded by the Renewal of Baptismal Vows, as on pages 276–8 of the *Alternative Service Book 1980*.

VII
A RITE OF DELIVERANCE (OR MINOR EXORCISM)

VII

A RITE OF DELIVERANCE (OR MINOR EXORCISM)
(South African)

(This form is a suggested outline for use where occult involvement is known or suspected, where there is some sort of spiritual oppression, or suspected possession of which one is uncertain.)

Instructions

1   Before entering upon this ministry the priest or lay person exercising it should prepare himself by prayer and self-examination.

2   No lay person shall enter upon this ministry without the knowledge and sanction of the priest, subject to any episcopal regulations.

3   The minister will often find it desirable to have other Christians present with him. They also should have prepared themselves.

4   All those present should promise not to make public any confidential matter revealed during the ministry, nor to break the seal of confession.

5   The person seeking ministry should be moved to penitence and encouraged to make a special confession of his sins before the priest if he has any serious matter upon his conscience.

6   The priest may need to give absolution during the ministry. A lay person exercising the ministry will not give absolution but will pray for God's forgiveness for the person.

7   The priest or minister should find out from the person beforehand the subjects for renunciation and for prayer, so that clear answers may be given to the questions asked in the service.

8   If it becomes evident after the use of this service that there is need for exorcism proper, the priest should consult the bishop. He must not, except in unavoidable emergency, make use of the rite of exorcism of persons without the bishop's authorization, and, even so, he must notify the bishop as soon as possible afterwards.

Introduction

Our Father in heaven,	Our Father, who art in heaven,
hallowed be your name,	hallowed be thy name;
your kingdom come,	thy kingdom come;
your will be done,	thy will be done;
on earth as in heaven.	on earth as it is in heaven.
Give us this day our daily bread.	Give us this day our daily bread.
Forgive us our sins	And forgive us our trespasses,
as we forgive those who sin	as we forgive those who trespass
against us.	against us.
Lead us not into temptation	And lead us not into temptation;
but deliver us from evil.	but deliver us from evil.
For the kingdom, the power and	For thine is the kingdom, the
the glory are yours	power, and the glory,
now and for ever. *Amen.*	for ever and ever. *Amen.*

Deliver us, merciful Lord, from all evils, past, present and to come, and grant us peace in our day. Keep us free from sin and safe from all distress, as we wait in joyful hope for the coming of our Saviour, Jesus Christ. *Amen.*

Confession

Let us call to mind and confess our sins.

Almighty God, our heavenly Father,
in penitence we confess that we have sinned against you
through our own fault
in thought, word and deed
and in what we have left undone.
For the sake of your Son, Christ our Lord,
forgive us all that is past
and grant that we may serve you in newness of life
to the glory of your Name. *Amen.*

Almighty God, who forgives all who truly repent, have mercy on you, pardon your sins and set you free from them; confirm and strengthen you in all goodness, and keep you in eternal life; through Jesus Christ our Lord. *Amen.*

Deliverance

Collect

God, your nature is always to have mercy and to forgive: loose your servant from every bond of evil and free *him* from all *his* sins. We ask this through Jesus Christ our Lord. *Amen.*

Reading

Hear, O Israel, the Lord our God is Lord alone and you shall love the Lord your God with all your heart, and with all your soul, and with all your mind, and with all your strength, and your neighbour as yourself (Mark 12.29–31).

Examination

The person seeking ministry should then be asked:

What are you wanting from God in his holy Church?

The person replies in his own words.

What will coming to Christ bring you?

The person replies in his own words.

Renunciation

The priest then calls on the person to turn to Christ and renounce Satan.

Do you renounce the devil and all the spiritual forces of wickedness that rebel against God?

I do.

Do you renounce the evil powers of this world which corrupt and destroy what God has created?

I do.

Do you renounce all sinful desires that draw you away from the love of God?

I do.

Do you renounce (*here specific mention is to be made of any occult practice in which the person may have been involved*)?

I do.

Stretching out his hands towards the person, the minister says:

Lord God of Hosts, before your presence the armies of hell are put to flight. Deliver *N.* from the assaults and temptations of the evil one. Free *him* from every evil and unclean spirit that may be assailing *him*. Strengthen and protect *him* by the power of your Holy Spirit; through Jesus Christ our Lord. *Amen.*

He may add the following rebuke:
Be gone, Satan, and cease to trouble this servant of God. In the Name of Jesus Christ. *Amen.*

Proclamation of Christ's lordship

The priest asks the person to proclaim Jesus as Lord, saying:

I want you to repeat after me: Jesus is Lord.

Jesus is Lord.

This may need to be repeated, and it may be sufficient to expel the evil spirit. In this case, end with thanksgiving and prayer after deliverance, as follows:

Thanksgiving and prayer after deliverance

Give thanks to the Lord, for he is gracious.

For his mercy endures for ever.

We praise you, Lord, that you have delivered your servant *N.* from these wicked spirits. Come to *him*, Lord, with the goodness and peace of your Son Jesus Christ, that *he* may have no fear, nor be troubled any more by the power of evil. We ask this through your Son Jesus Christ, our Saviour and Redeemer. *Amen.*

After a period of silent or extempore prayer, the minister may lay his hands upon the person and say:

Deliverance

May our Lord Jesus Christ himself, and God our Father, who loved us and in his grace has given us unfailing courage and a firm hope, encourage and comfort you, that you may always do and say what is good. May the Lord who is faithful strengthen you, and keep you safe from the evil one. And now may the Lord of peace himself give you peace at all times and in every way (2 Thess. 2.16–17; 3.3–5, 16).

And the blessing of God Almighty, the Father, the Son and the Holy Spirit, be among you and remain with you always. *Amen.*

VIII

THE RITE OF EXORCISM OF PERSONS (MAJOR EXORCISM)

A major exorcism of a person should not be carried out without the express permission of the bishop of the diocese, who should be notified individually of every case in which it is proposed that this ministry should be exercised. It should only be carried out by persons having the authority of the bishop to do so. For that reason it is not necessary to include the appropriate rite in this publication. Those with a bona fide reason for requiring to have a copy of the service should consult the Christian Exorcism Study Group or their diocesan adviser in this ministry.

IX

SOME PRAYERS AND DEVOTIONS FOR PRIVATE OR LITURGICAL USE
(taken from the South African material referred to on page 120 above)

Eternal Lord God,
you created the holy angels to worship and serve you:
Grant that in their ceaseless combat against demonic powers
they may guard and strengthen us in the fight against these powers on
    earth;
through Jesus Christ our Lord. *Amen.*

Holy Father,
your Son kept his apostles safe by the power of your Name.

132

Keep us safe from the wiles of the evil one,
and consecrate us to yourself, through Jesus Christ our Lord. *Amen.*

Protect us, Lord Jesus, by the power of your Name
and by your precious blood which was shed upon the cross.
Send your holy angels to guard and defend us.
Uphold us with the prayers of your saints.
Be with us, Lord, for you have cast down Satan by your death
and have risen in triumph
and have promised to abide with us always, even to the end of time.
Amen.

Almighty God,
your Son Jesus Christ gave power to his apostles
to heal the sick and to cast out demons:
Pardon our sins and grant us the strength of faith and the power of your
    Spirit
that we may come against these evil spirits with boldness and safety;
through your Son Jesus Christ our Lord. *Amen.*

Thanks be to God:

Who gives us the victory through our Lord Jesus Christ
(1 Cor. 15.57).

Now the salvation and the power and the Kingdom of our God, and the
authority of his Christ have come:

For the accuser of our brethren has been thrown down (Rev.
12.10).

The Lord of Hosts is with us:

The God of Jacob is our refuge (Ps. 46.7).

Glory and honour and power are yours by right, O Lamb who was slain:

For by your blood you have ransomed men for God (Rev. 5.12,
9).

Behold the cross of Christ and flee, you powers of darkness!

The Lion of Judah, the root of David, has conquered.

Deliverance

Lord Jesus Christ, to whom all power in heaven and earth is given, in your Name alone is salvation. Cleanse the heart of your servant *N.*; grant that the Holy Spirit may dwell in *him*, to turn *his* body to your purpose, *his* will to your obedience, and *his* affections to your love. *Amen.*

Almighty God, heavenly Father,
breathe your Holy Spirit into the heart of this your servant *N.*;
inspire *him* with love for goodness and truth;
May *he*, fearing only to be faithless, have no other fear;
May *he*, knowing your Fatherhood, be ever mindful of your love;
May *he*, in serving you faithfully until death, live eternally with you;
through Jesus Christ our Lord. *Amen.*

St Patrick's Breastplate

Christ be with me, Christ within me,
Christ behind me, Christ before me,
Christ beside me, Christ to win me,
Christ to comfort and restore me.
Christ beneath me, Christ above me,
Christ in quiet, Christ in danger,
Christ in hearts of all that love me,
Christ in mouth of friend and stranger.

I bind unto myself the Name,
The strong Name of the Trinity;
By invocation of the same,
The Three in One and One in Three.
Of whom all nature hath creation;
Eternal Father, Spirit, Word:
Praise to the Lord of my salvation,
Salvation is of Christ the Lord. *Amen.*

Jesus,
May all that is you flow into me;
May your Body and your Blood be my food and my drink;
May your passion and death be my strength and my life;
May the shelter I seek be the shadow of your cross;
Let me not run from the love which you offer,
But hold me safe from the forces of evil.

On each of my dyings shed your light and your love.
Keep calling me until that day comes
when with your saints I may praise you for ever. *Amen.*

A form of blessing

May the risen and ascended Christ, mightier than the hordes of hell, more glorious than the heavenly hosts, be with you in all your ways. *Amen.*

May his cross protect you by day and by night, at all times and in all places. *Amen.*

May he guard and deliver you from the snares of the devil, from the assaults of evil spirits, from the wrath of the wicked, from all base passions, and from the fear of the known and of the unknown. *Amen.*

May the saints of God pray for you, and the angels of God guard and protect you. *Amen.*

And may the Lord of heaven and earth grant you freedom from your sins, and all the riches of his grace. *Amen.*

The blessing of God almighty, the Father, the Son and the Holy Spirit, be upon you and remain with you always. *Amen.*

A litany

Remember not, Lord, our offences, nor the offences of our forefathers, and do not condemn us for our sins.

Lord, have mercy.	**Lord, have mercy.**
Christ, have mercy.	**Christ, have mercy.**
Lord, have mercy.	**Lord, have mercy.**
Heavenly Father,	**Have mercy on him.**
Jesus, Redeemer of the world,	**Have mercy on him.**
Holy Spirit, Comforter,	**Have mercy on him.**
Holy Trinity, one God,	**Have mercy on him.**

Deliverance

From all evil,	**Good Lord, deliver him.**
From all sin,	**Good Lord, deliver him.**
From your wrath,	**Good Lord, deliver him.**
From sudden and unprepared death,	**Good Lord, deliver him.**
From all the snares and assaults of the devil,	**Good Lord, deliver him.**
From worldliness and love of money,	**Good Lord, deliver him.**
From anger, hatred and malice,	**Good Lord, deliver him.**
From arrogance, pride and hypocrisy,	**Good Lord, deliver him.**
From envy and all uncharitableness,	**Good Lord, deliver him.**
From fornication and adultery,	**Good Lord, deliver him.**
From gluttony and sloth,	**Good Lord, deliver him.**
From all spiritual blindness and unbelief,	**Good Lord, deliver him.**
From all false teaching,	**Good Lord, deliver him.**
From all the deceits of the world, the flesh and the devil,	**Good Lord, deliver him.**
From everlasting death,	**Good Lord, deliver him.**
By the mystery of your holy incarnation,	**Good Lord, deliver him.**
By your baptism, fasting and temptation,	**Good Lord, deliver him.**
By your mighty acts of power,	**Good Lord, deliver him.**
By your preaching of the Kingdom,	**Good Lord, deliver him.**
By your cross and passion,	**Good Lord, deliver him.**

By your death and burial,	**Good Lord, deliver him.**
By your mighty resurrection,	**Good Lord, deliver him.**
By your glorious ascension,	**Good Lord, deliver him.**
By the coming of the Holy Spirit,	**Good Lord, deliver him.**
By your everlasting intercession,	**Good Lord, deliver him.**
In the day of judgement,	**Good Lord, deliver him.**

Lord, give *him* peace.	**Hear us, good Lord.**
In your mercy and your pity, guard and protect *him*.	**Hear us, good Lord.**
Look upon *him* in your love and restore *him*.	**Hear us, good Lord.**
Reach out and rescue *him* from *his* tribulations and attacks.	**Hear us, good Lord.**
Bless this your servant *N*., and deliver *him*.	**Hear us, good Lord.**
Snatch *him* from the grasp of the evil one.	**Hear us, good Lord.**
Deliver *him* from all demonic assaults.	**Hear us, good Lord.**

Christ, hear us.	**Christ, graciously hear us.**
Lamb of God, you take away the sins of the world;	**Have mercy on him.**
Lamb of God, you take away the sins of the world;	**Have mercy on him.**
Lamb of God, you take away the sins of the world;	**Give him your peace.**

Remember not, Lord, our offences, nor the offences of our forefathers, and do not condemn us for our sins.

Deliverance

The Lord's Prayer

Deliver us, merciful Lord, from all evils past, present and to come,
and grant us peace in our day.
Keep us free from sin and safe from all distress
As we wait in joyful hope for the coming of our Saviour, Jesus Christ.
Amen.

X

SOME SUITABLE PSALMS AND PASSAGES OF SCRIPTURE FOR THE MINISTRY OF DELIVERANCE
(taken from the South African material referred to on page 120 above)

Psalms

3; 12; 22; 31; 35; 46; 68; 70; 71.1–11; 86; 91.

Gospels

Matthew 4.23–5	Jesus healing every kind of trouble
Matthew 9.32–3	The dumb demoniac
Matthew 15.21–8	The Canaanite woman's daughter
Mark 1.21–8	The man in the synagogue
Mark 3.7–12	Healing by Lake Galilee
Mark 6.7–13	The mission of the Twelve
Mark 9.14–29	The demonized epileptic boy
Mark 16.14–20	Signs following those who believe
Luke 4.40–41	Healing at eventide
Luke 8.26–39	Legion
Luke 10.16–20	The return of the seventy disciples
Luke 11.14–22	Jesus casting out demons by the power of the Spirit
John 12.27–32	The overthrow of the prince of this world
John 19.17–30	'It is finished' – the crucifixion.

Other New Testament readings

Acts 5.12–16	Miracles and wonders of the Apostles
Acts 8.4–8	Philip in Samaria

Acts 16.16–18	The girl exorcized by Paul
Acts 19.11–20	The sons of Sceva
Ephesians 6.10–17	The armour of God
1 John 5.12–21	The safety of the child of God
Revelation 1.12–18	Vision of Christ
Revelation 12.1–9	The overthrow of the dragon
Revelation 20.1–3	The binding of Satan.

Index